# Writing on the Job

## Faster, Better, and Smarter

By Dona J. Young
February 11, 2013
Copyright © Writer's Toolkit Publishing LLC


Cover designed by Nanc Ashby
www.saveldesign.com

ISBN-13: 978-1482520460
ISBN-10: 148252046X

Printed in the United States.
This book is printed on acid-free paper.

Writer's Toolkit Publishing LLC
www.wtkpublishing.com

# Writing on the Job

## Faster, Better, and Smarter

**Dona J. Young**

To Sally and Helen

# Brief Contents

# Introduction

*Writing on the Job* is for professionals who want to bring their writing to a higher level so that they thrive on the job. Though no magic bullet exists, this book walks you through a process so that you develop expert skills in a straightforward and painless way.

As you integrate leading-edge practices for writing and communication into your daily activities, you reap excellent dividends. By becoming more efficient, you save time; by becoming more effective, you enhance relationships.

In fact, e-writing is as much about developing relationships as about conveying information. That is because most jobs get done, at least in part, based on the quality of the relationships among the players. By tuning in to diverse styles, you improve your ability to build strong client relationships, an underlying purpose of business writing that is often not fully developed.

Most professionals have not learned how to edit effectively, and the cost is high—from wasted time to lost credibility. Effective editing takes the mystery out of how to produce writing that gets results. In each chapter, you learn core principles that enhance your skills so that you produce credible writing that is clear and concise. By the end, you may find writing to be a rewarding activity that shapes your thinking as well as your life and career.

This brief book introduces you to essential principles that are more fully developed in *A Guide for Business Writing: Write to Learn—Edit to Clarify,* which contains exercises along with keys. For interactive exercises, go to **www.youngcommunication.com** and click on the *Learning Activities* tab. Now *go for it*!

# Contents

## Part 2: Write Better

### Chapter 4   Control the Core   39

### Chapter 5   Don't *Pause* for Commas   51

## Chapter 6   Keep Verbs Alive and Active   73

# Part 3: Write Smarter

# 1

# Embrace the Process

You have spent a big chunk of your time and education learning how to write well, so what can you learn now to write *faster*, *better*, and *smarter*?

First, let's talk about how you can **write faster**. Writing is a process, but you may not be using it to your advantage. For example, do your ideas seem to dissolve before they hit the page? Do you focus on the *result*, editing your writing while the words are still in your head? Learn about the process and embrace it—use planning tools to get your ideas down fast and organize them effectively. When you give your reader easy access to your message, you also receive faster and more thorough responses.

To **write better**, develop strong editing skills so that you base decisions on *principles* rather than *guesses*. For example, if you are looking for the *right pause* to place a comma, you are likely to feel confused every time that you write: commas are *not* placed on the basis of pauses, but the myth is more prevalent than the truth. If that is your approach, you are no doubt making many errors, some involving semicolons; you see, fear of semicolons is common among writers who use the pause approach.

Though punctuation is the key to developing expert editing skills, punctuation is only one tool in your editing arsenal. Other tools include *active* and *passive voice, viewpoint, tone, conciseness,* and *formatting*, each of which helps you connect with your reader and get your point across effectively.

To **write smarter**, focus on *purpose* and *context*: revise your writing so that your reader gets maximum value with minimum effort. When readers have an easy time understanding your meaning, you make their day run more smoothly. You also make it easier for them to respond to you and your requests.

As for *context*, keep in mind that an underlying purpose of business writing is to *enhance the relationship*:

- Connect to your reader as one human to another—that's a critical part of how the job gets done.

Right now, you may focus most of your attention on conveying information, which is natural. However, by shifting your focus to your reader, you may spend less energy to accomplish more.

Most professionals have not learned how to edit effectively, and it costs them in a multitude of ways, from wasted time to lost credibility. However, by learning a few core principles, you can improve the skills that you use daily to save time and achieve effective results.

Though each chapter helps you write faster, better, and smarter, the tools in this chapter and the next give insight into how to produce more in less time. So let's get started.


## Editor's Block

Writing is difficult for everyone at times, and knowing why it is difficult can help you keep your creative energy flowing. For example, when you avoid writing or cannot produce new work, that's *writer's block*. Professional writers confront writer's block, but business writers are more likely to confront *editor's block*.

Editor's block is not only more common than writer's block, it creates far more havoc for those who write daily on the job. To find out if you have editor's block, ask yourself if you:

- Figure things out in your head before putting words on the page.
- Correct grammar, punctuation, and spelling as you compose.
- Lose your thoughts before getting them on the page.
- Send out messages without proofreading or editing them first.

If any of the above apply, see if you can diagnose which type of editor's block fits your profile:

- *Editor's Block Type A*: You edit as you compose, and your ideas get jammed in your head or dissolve before they reach the page.

- *Editor's Block Type B:* You do not proofread or edit your work before you send it out. Since you are unsure of what to correct or revise, you hold your breath and press the *send* button.

Even if you have both types, do not despair. To take care of **Editor's Block Type A**, separate composing from editing: you will see an immediate difference in your writing. You will produce more in less time; you will also feel less frustrated and, ultimately, more confident. The planning and composing tools in this chapter will help you with this type of editing block. However, you must remain steadfast in your new process, as you are breaking a long-held habit.

To overcome **Editor's Block Type B**, you need to take the time to proofread and edit each piece of writing that you produce. By developing your skills, you will understand the principles that lead to correct, clear, and concise writing. Then be vigilant as you edit your writing.

Taking care of Editor's Block Type B is not as challenging as you may fear—this book covers editing principles step by step, one principle at a time.

Your first step in this process, out of necessity, is to *separate composing from editing.* When you compose freely, the thinking behind your writing takes center stage, allowing you to reach insight to solve problems—your purpose for writing in the first place.

Core editing principles give you clear-cut answers that take the mystery out of how to produce effective writing. As you edit, you reach clarity; but more important, you shape your writing for your readers so that it gets right to the point in a clear and concise style.

## Planning Tools and Templates

When you compose, you are drawing from your creative side; when you edit, you are drawing on your analytical skills. When you edit as you compose, feeling stuck is the natural outcome.

Use the planning tools discussed here to get your ideas down freely and in a format so that you can organize them easily.

Mind Maps    Mind mapping allows you to get your ideas on the page in a quick, spontaneous way. First, choose your topic. Next, write your topic in the middle of the page, circling it. Finally, free associate ideas and cluster them around your topic. (See Figure 1.1 on page 5.)

If you have great ideas but cannot seem to get them on the page before they dissolve, mind mapping is your solution.

**Figure 1.1 | Mind Map:** What is difficult about writing?

*Once you select your topic, spend about 3 minutes getting your ideas on the page: no pauses, no corrections, no criticism.*

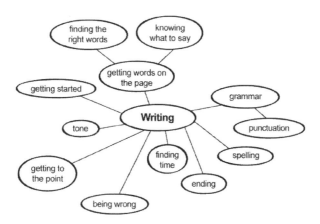

Experiment creating a mind map of a current task; spend about 3 minutes working on your mind map.

- Does a visual map give you a global understanding of your topic?
- Can you organize your ideas easily now that they are on the page?
- Do you feel more energized to take action?

You may also consider experimenting with mind maps to use as a daily time-management tool and to keep you organized when you leave voicemail messages.

- **Time Management Tool**. Write the date in the middle of the page and then quickly jot down your *to-do list*. As you branch out, leave space for details.

- **Voicemail Messages**. Develop an organized pattern for leaving voicemail messages. Mind map your message by writing down your key points and then apply the following pattern:

  o Give your name and number.
  o State your key points, include due dates.
  o Repeat your number slowly.

If you prefer mind mapping on your computer, many mind-mapping applications are available free: search, "mind mapping tools free."

Page Maps    After you create your mind map, put key points along the side of a page. Then use each key point as a *side heading*; fill in the detail, with the familiar to new information. (See Figure 1.2 below.)

**Figure 1.2 | Page Map: The Benefits of Product X**

*When creating a page map, use the information from your skeleton outline or mind map as a starting point and then fill in the details.*

---

The Benefits of Product X

Introduction (define the product)

**Part 1: Analyzing the Need**

Audience

Competition

**Part 2: Marketing Plan**

Developing a Brand

Creating a Logo

Sales Materials

**Part 3: Distributing the Product**

Conclusion

A *page map* gives you a skeleton of your ideas mapped on the page. By starting with side headings that a page map provides, writing becomes a building process. This technique is perfect for long projects, such as writing a report or even a book. A page map gives you a head start because you are not facing a blank page.

By experimenting with a page map, you are more likely to start using side headings in your everyday writing, adding a formatting element that makes your message appealing and accessible. Even at a glance, readers know where to find specific information.

Fishbone Diagrams   A fishbone diagram is a *root-cause analysis* that forces deep probing into a problem.

Though a fish-bone diagram addresses multiple components of a problem or project, you can simplify the format and use it as a daily problem-solving tool; you can even use it when you journal.

- First, identify the problem.
- Next, if your problem has individual components, list them.
- Finally, for each component, ask *why* five times.

For example, let's say you are having difficulty completing a writing task. Start by writing a problem statement and then work through it.

**Problem statement:** I am having difficulty writing this report.

*Why?*   I am having trouble getting started.
*Why?*   I am feeling as if it is out of my control.
*Why?*   I don't understand the topic well enough.
*Why?*   I haven't done my research.
*Why?*   I haven't taken the time to find resources.

Finally, define your **next step**:  Do research today from 3 to 4 p.m.

If you are working with a team on a project, take a formal approach by breaking your project into its component parts and probing each part. For example, many projects include the following components: people, process, materials, equipment, environment, management.

You can find templates for fishbone diagrams online; simply do a search, "fishbone (diagram) templates."

Templates    Use a template during the composing or revising stage of writing for documents of any length. The template you use will vary based on the type of writing you are doing.

An example of a generic template is the **PEAR** template. Here are the elements of the model:

**P**    *Purpose:* make *key points* instantly accessible.

**E**    *Evidence, explanations, examples:* support key points, as needed.

**A**    *Actions and appreciation:* list actions you or your reader need to take; show your client appreciation.

**R**    *Recommendations and recap*: draw conclusions for the reader.

As you compose, use the PEAR model to create *side headings* or to map your page. By breaking down each part based on purpose, the PEAR template ensures that you have developed all relevant aspects of a document.

For a task that involves problem  solving, use the **ISAT** template:

| | | |
|---|---|---|
| **I** | **Issue** | What *issue* or problem are you working on? |
| **S** | **Solution** | What is the *solution* or what are the options? |
| **A** | **Action** | What *actions* need to be taken and by whom? |
| **T** | **Thanks** | Do you need to include a word of *thanks*? |

For e-mail, use the **CAET** template:

| | | |
|---|---|---|
| **C** | **Connect** | Connect with your reader, creating a personal link. |
| **A** | **Act** | State action needed at the beginning of the message. |
| **E** | **Explain** | Include only details relevant to your reader. |
| **T** | **Thank** | Thank your client . . . everyone likes to be appreciated. |

If you loosely apply a template as you compose, your content will be somewhat structured before you revise. Use template elements as *side headings* to create a page map as you rough out your ideas. In addition, analyze the kinds of reports that you do, and then *create your own template.*

## Composing Tools

The first critical step to improving your process involves writing freely so that you can edit effectively. To separate composing from editing, freewrite daily. Freewriting will help you shut your critic so that your critical voices do not shut down your creative process.

Freewriting     As you freewrite (or *free type*, if you prefer), you are learning to compose freely while blocking the compulsion to correct your writing. Transfer your thoughts directly from your head to the page without filtering them.

Set the clock for 10 minutes and start writing. Since writing is a problem-solving activity, you may find yourself actively working through problems that cause stress. Freewriting clears the head so that you gain insight, renew your energy, and improve your focus.

Focused Writing    In contrast to the random thoughts of freewriting, focused writing involves only one topic. Once you choose a topic, write about only that topic for about 10 minutes or 3 pages.

Focused writing helps you make good use of small amounts of time that would otherwise be lost. Focused writing can also help you jump-start a project that you have been avoiding.

---

**COACHING TIP:**

**Use *Signal Anxiety* to Your Benefit**

*Signal anxiety* is a healthy type of anxiety that tugs at your sleeve, gently reminding you to start working. However, rather working on an unimportant task to relieve your feelings, take action on the task that you are avoiding, the one that has the impending deadline. You will feel instant relief and see immediate results.

As you take action, do not try to start from the beginning. Write about what you know first. Let what you already know lead you to fresh insights. In fact, once you start writing, you gain deeper insight, even when you are not thinking about your topic.

Writing forces you to make progress by pulling you to deeper levels of understanding. That is why writing sometimes feels painful: putting critical thoughts on paper takes energy and courage because you force yourself to take positions, make decisions, and think clearly.

Writing is a problem-solving activity: writing is *thinking on paper*. Trust the process.

---

# E-Time Management

Improving the way that you manage e-mail will save you time and energy. Make it your goal to develop a *system*: a toolbox of decisions that support you in getting your job done.

As you review the following suggestions, remain open to trying them before you decide they will not work.[1]

1.  **Reduce interruptions**. Take back control of your focus and workflow: stop checking your messages *on demand*.

    o  Turn off your mail alert indicator.

    o  Identify set times to check your messages.

    If you need to check messages often, try limiting yourself to checking once an hour or even once every half hour. When an issue is top priority, the phone is the best solution, regardless of whether you are sending a request of responding to one.

    By staying focused on only one task, you will achieve more in less time. That is because *multi-tasking does not work*—your brain can really focus on only one task at a time. If you now think that multi-tasking works, it is because you are able to switch back and forth between tasks quickly; but when you do so, you are more vulnerable to making mistakes.[2] By switching back and forth, you lose time because you also lose focus.

2.  **Read and respond, and then delete or file**. Try to handle each message only once.

    o  When a message needs a simple response, respond as soon as you read the message.

    o  If you need to take action, file the message until you can complete the requested task.

3. **Create folders**. At a minimum, create folders for *action* and *reference*.

   o **Action** messages require a time commitment, which you may need to plan into your day.

   o **Reference** messages add clutter to your Inbox: after you have responded, file them so that you have the history or documentation, as needed.

   o *Note:* If you will not be able to complete the task within a day or two, send a quick message letting the other know when to expect your response.

4. **Set boundaries.** Identify the issues that drain your energy or time, and head them off at the pass; for example:

   o Do not scan e-mail when you do not have the time to respond.

   o Do not send late-night messages *when you can avoid it.*

   o Set a limit for the number of times you exchange messages about a topic before making a phone call—3 or 4 times?

   When an issue is urgent or you are not getting the response that you need, call your client.

5. **Suggest rather than ask vague or open-ended questions.**

   o If you are scheduling a meeting, offer the reader two or three possible times, adding a comment, "If none of these work for you, let me know a time or two that would."

   o Propose solutions by saying, "I suggest that . . ." or "Would it work for you to . . . ?"

6. **Bring your Inbox down to zero.** Though time management experts recommend this, only you can determine if this is a

viable option for you; then decide when and how often you will do this: once a day . . . once a week . . . once a quarter?

- o Develop your filing system by adding the folders you need.
- o Handle each message only once.
- o Read and respond then file or delete.

If you find it impossible to delete messages and your Inbox gets too full, you can also move all of your messages to a folder labeled, "Old Messages." You will have brought your Inbox to zero but still retain the security blanket and ease of finding whatever you need.

To increase productivity, apply the following time-management tips:

- Keep a *to-do list*, using software to keep you organized. For free software, Google "software for getting organized."
- Complete challenging tasks during the time of day when you make your best decisions—in other words, when you feel fresh.
- Set internal deadlines so that you meet external demands.
- And remember, multi-tasking does not work.

Finally, reflect on the voices that might be holding you back.

## Critical Voices

Writing is difficult, and all writers face what they feel to be insurmountable roadblocks—that is, until they write their way out of them. Then, in retrospect, what first seemed to be impossible turns into a deeper understanding and a better solution.

The creative part of the self is hypersensitive. When you criticize yourself, you effectively drain your energy and motivation, not only sabotaging your passion but possibly also your life's mission.

Shutting down your inner critic is more difficult than dealing with criticism from others. When someone criticizes you or your work, the worst part is that it triggers self-criticism. In fact, you may even be using criticism from years past that is no longer true (and that may never have been true) to sabotage your writing today.

When you feel critical of yourself or others, write about it. As you write about your fears and feelings, you process them so that you do not become stuck, feeling like a victim. As an ancient saying reminds us, "If you hold it in, it will destroy you; if you let it out, it will free you."

In her book *Loving What Is*, Byron Katie advises that the way to deal with negative thoughts is to challenge them.[3] The next time you have a negative thought or start telling yourself a negative story, ask yourself, "Is that true?" Then ask again, "Is that really true?"

Most negative thoughts are opinions, and opinions are not facts. If you cannot prove that a negative thought is true, let it go. Even if you can prove that it is true, it is still possible to let it go: staying positive is a decision leading to less stress resulting in better health.

Your first step is becoming aware, your second step is claiming ownership, and your third step is empowering yourself to change: *name it, claim it, and change it.*

Also, be aware that an unconscious fear of criticism is worse than criticism itself: once you hear the actual words, you can regroup and emerge stronger. In contrast, fear is paralyzing, and the only way to combat fear is to take action.

Start writing, even if you are writing only about your fears. As you write freely, your ideas flow. Your topic takes on a life of its own, becoming ever larger as you follow your insights; even subtle insights can lead to profound changes. Show up and trust the process.

Fear of criticism goes hand in hand with an expectation of perfection. When you are disappointed with yourself for not being perfect, you are setting yourself up for failure:

*Perfect writing does not exist.*

Ernest Hemmingway faced his fears by saying,

> Do not worry. You have always written before and you will write now. All you have to do is write one true sentence. Write the truest sentence that you know.[4]

Perfection exists only in the mind, so do not beat yourself up for being human. Stay ahead of the game by expecting challenges and even embracing them.

## Knowledge Gaps

While writing is more of an art, editing is more of a science. When you write, you draw upon critical and creative thinking skills to gain insight into the problem that you are solving. However, when you edit, you draw upon mechanical skills. Because editing draws upon learned skill sets, editing should be easier than composing. Unless, however, you have knowledge gaps in some of the mechanical skills—and most writers do.

When writing feels frustrating, consider if a knowledge gap is keeping you from making progress. As you work through this book, you systematically fill any knowledge gaps that you may have in skill sets needed to write correctly and edit effectively.

In fact, if you now separate composing from editing, you have already filled a critical knowledge gap: embracing the writing process is the first hurdle to overcome in becoming an effective editor.

By working on core principles that lead to clear, correct, and concise writing, you will bring the quality of your writing to a higher level. As you review each principle, apply it to your own writing. Learning involves patience to see progress, courage to try new ways of doing things, and motivation to keep working toward a goal.

Writing is a powerful learning tool because writing leads to insight and takes thinking to deeper levels. For example, have you ever noticed that you can think about the same problem all day, only to end up feeling drained and helpless? In contrast, once you start writing, you either solve your problem or release it so that you return to the present; and in the process, you become energized. That's one reason why writing—even business writing—is magical.

## Recap

By separating composing from editing, you produce more in less time. As you compose, shut down your critic so that you can hear your voice.

Writing is a problem-solving activity. Find clarity and focus by writing until you are clearheaded. The more you write, the stronger your skills become: practice makes progress. If you write between 10 to 20 minutes daily (or until you fill 2 to 3 pages), you will achieve your goals and work toward solving problems. To *up the ante*, consider writing your memoir, one experience at a time.

If you cannot write daily, write at least 4 times a week. Start your day by doing a mind map; use this planning tool to organize and prioritize your projects and time. After you complete a mind map, create a page map so that you do not face a blank page.

When you feel *signal anxiety*, take action. Taking action is the only antidote to procrastination, which is equivalent to *fear of the unknown*. Taking the first step is equivalent to taking a giant leap.

## Action Steps

What are your *takeaways*? What key points do you plan to apply?

## References

1.  *Email Time and Task Management*, http://www.priacta.com/Articles/ Email_Time_Management.shtml, accessed on August 24, 2012.

2.  Steve Nguyen, *Multitasking Doesn't Work*, Workplace Psychology, http://workplacepsychology.net/2011/04/04/multitasking-doesnt-work, accessed on February 1, 2013.

3.  Byron Katie, *Loving What Is: Four Questions That Can Change Your Life*, Three Rivers Press, New York, 2003.

4.  Larry W. Phillips, Editor, *Ernest Hemingway on Writing*, Scribner, New York, 1984, page 28.

# 2

# Put Purpose First

Not all information carries the same weight, and this can be a hard lesson to learn. For example, an English professor shared that the best criticism he ever received on his writing was from one of his professors in graduate school, who commented:

> "The problem is, you don't know the difference between what is important and what isn't."

Though this feedback was challenging to process, the professor also revealed that, as a result, he changed his writing and ultimately his decision-making process. He even used the lesson to clarify his values and make other changes.

Do you take the time to revise your writing until readers have immediate access to what is important, making your purpose readily accessible? *Purpose provides context*, making detail meaningful.

Think of purpose this way: people want to know the destination before they hear the fine points of how to get there. In fact, most of the time, readers do not care how you arrived at your conclusions. They want to get to the bottom line as quickly as possible.

You see, when readers do not understand where comments are leading, they have difficulty understanding details and lose their motivation to continue reading. However, they are eager to know what you need from them so that they can move to their next task.

## What Is Important?

When you edit, make your purpose directly accessible for your readers by asking:

- What is the most important issue?
- What are my outcomes and conclusions?
- What action do I want the reader to take?

Provide readers with the outcome, not the *how come*. When you edit, move your *end point* to the beginning, making it your first point. Most important, make it clear what you need from your readers so that they can respond.

Therefore, analyze the detail in your message. Though that detail led you to your insights and conclusions, that same detail may be counter-productive for your readers. As Mark Twain once said,

"The more you explain it, the more I don't understand it."

## Purpose and Process

Understanding purpose often comes as a flash of insight as you compose. Once you write a sentence that clarifies what you want to say, use your insight as a signal that you are ready to start editing.

1. Cut and paste the key sentence to the beginning of your message.
2. Then delete unnecessary, irrelevant detail.

Writing is a discovery process: as your thinking becomes clear, your purpose becomes clear. However, as you write, avoid using the word *purpose*. For example, your first draft might include the following:

My purpose for writing you is to find out what I need to do to open an account.

When you revise your message, remove the word *purpose*:

I would like to know the process for opening an account.

As you read the following e-mail, take special note of where in the message the writer's purpose finally becomes clear.

---

Dear Ms. Holloway:

My name is Donald Draper, and I recently attended a local job fair where I met an associate of yours who was representing your company at the job fair. His name is Roger Sterling, and he suggested that I write you because you are the person in charge of the intern program at your company. To give you a little background about myself, I am currently completing my degree at Best College, and I am scheduled to receive my degree in marketing next spring. My purpose in writing you is to find out if you have any openings in your intern program this coming winter. I would be pleased to send you my resume or come in for an interview at your earliest convenience. I look forward to hearing from you.

Sincerely,

Donald Draper

---

**Before you turn the page, trying revising the above message:**

1. Identify the key point.
2. Bring it to the beginning of the message.
3. Cut irrelevant information.

## Put Your Bottom Line Up Front

- Make key points instantly accessible.
- Your reader should see your purpose *at a glance*.

**Here is a revision with the key point up front:**

---

Dear Ms. Holloway:

At a recent job fair, Roger Sterling suggested that I write you about a possible opening in your intern program this winter.

I will receive my degree in marketing from Best College this spring; my résumé is attached.

I look forward to hearing from you. In the meantime, you can reach me at 202-555-1212.

Best regards,

Donald Draper

---

*Was the revised message more accessible? How did the tone change? What other changes improved the message?*

Composing is messy; editing is the tidying up part. At times, you will need to cut and paste a key sentence to the beginning of a paragraph; at other times, you will need to cut and paste a key paragraph to another part of your document.

## The Value Test

Every sentence in your document should hold value for your reader—so as you edit, take your reader's perspective and ask:

- Does that matter?
- What is the value, the benefit?

If a sentence does not contain new information or add substance, cut it. As you read each sentence, ask "So what?"[1]

Another value test is to reflect on how your comments may relate to feelings—yours and your readers, especially in e-mail. For example, whenever you seem to get some sort of satisfaction or emotional release from making a comment, you might be better off leaving it out: *when in doubt, leave it out.*

---

**It's *Not* about You: It's about Your Client's Goals.**

- How can your expertise *benefit your client*?
- What *value* do you offer your client?

---

## Reader Expectations

In part, you can tune in to what your readers expect by identifying what *you* expect and value.

In longer documents or speeches, ask yourself if your readers are experts or novices. Experts expect technical details. However, a general audience does not relate well to a lot of specific detail.

If you are writing an e-mail, you are not likely to lose a reader for too little detail (unless you are rude or abrupt). When readers do not get enough detail, they ask for what they need. However, you can lose a reader in a nanosecond by filling an e-mail with unnecessary details. Too much information (TMI) leads some readers to save the long-winded message until later, but later may never arrive.

When you write about unfamiliar topics, your writing is more likely to sound complicated. That is partly because you do not yet understand your topic well enough to present complex information in a simple way. Writing about a topic is the best way to learn about it because writing leads to clarity.

Many professionals erroneously think that they sound smarter when their writing is complicated. However, readers connect easily with writing that is alive and in the moment and written in a clear, direct voice. Therefore, once you have drafted your idea, edit your writing until your words on the page sound as fluent as they would if you were speaking:

*If you would not say it that way, do not write it that way.*

If your writing now sounds complicated, consider if you are trying to impress your readers. In other words, do you use a word such as *utilization* when you could use its simpler version, *use*? Also, canned phrases, such as *attached please find* and *per your request*, sound artificial. Would you ever sit across from someone at lunch and say, "Per your request . . . . "?

If you use your speech as a guide, simple writing will become natural. By the way, to avoid using *per your request*, simply say, *as you requested*; instead of *attached please find*, simply say, *attached is*. (See Chapter 8, *Be Concise*, for suggestions on using simple, concise language.)

Follow Leonardo DaVinci's advice when he said:

"Simplicity is the ultimate sophistication."

On the other hand, perhaps you have fallen into the opposite writing habit, which is that your writing sounds too informal. For example, do you use slang, incorrect grammar, or text-messaging language? If that is the case, work through editing principles until you bring your skills to level at which you would feel confident writing to anyone.

To improve your writing, write freely and frequently; to improve your final product, build strong editing skills. The way to become an incurable editor is to work on one core principle at a time—each time that you apply principle to practice, you reach deeper levels of clarity.

## Recap

By writing freely, you gain insight so that you state your purpose clearly. Once you have written the sentence that best describes your purpose, cut and paste it to the beginning of your message. Then cut irrelevant information, and your key point will stand out.

Edit your writing until it is correct, clear, and concise. As Albert Einstein once said,

"Everything should be made as simple as possible, but not simpler."

Write first for yourself, and then edit for your reader. Give yourself time to process your topic so that when you return to your writing, you can simplify it.

Stepping away from your writing is a critical element of editing and revising. In fact, nothing can substitute for time in reaching clarity: just as writing is a process, so is thinking.

## Action Steps

What are your *takeaways*? What key points do you plan to apply?

_____

_____

_____

_____

_____

_____

## Reference

1.  Jane Curry and Diana Young, *Be a Brilliant Business Writer*, Ten Speed Press, New York, 2010.

# 3

# Respect the Reader

Respect starts with small courtesies, such as proofreading for typos, and includes grander actions, such as editing for brevity.

By making it easy for your reader to understand your message, you are making it easy for your reader to respond to your message quickly and, hopefully, in kind.

This chapter provides guidelines for communicating to a broad range of readers who have diverse styles. By following these best practices, you are less likely to send negative *micro-messages*, also discussed in this chapter. By the way, a *micro-message* is a message *hidden between the lines* and may be sent unintentionally. At times, the unspoken micro-message has more impact on your reader than the actual words of your message.

By following the guidelines presented here, you can speak to a broad audience with confidence. In addition, you learn more about diverse *communication styles* in Chapter 10, *Be Sensitive to Diverse Styles*, as well as Chapter 15, *Apply Best Practices*.

All professional writing occurs in the context of relationship. By presenting your message in the clearest, easiest way for your reader to respond, you enhance the relationship.

Let us start by walking through the various parts of an e-mail message to identify how to connect with readers effectively.

# Create a Personal Link

One of the issues with e-communication is that writers get lost behind the screen, forgetting the human elements of communication. By using a salutation and a closing, you help reinforce a personal link between you and your reader, reminding both of you that you are one person speaking to another.

Salutations     Even if you write to someone often, use a salutation with the first message you exchange for the day. For example, use the name of the recipient, preceding it with the word *hi* or *hello*, if you wish. However, if you do not know your recipient well or prefer to be formal, use the word *dear*. Any variations of the following are acceptable business salutations:

| | | |
|---|---|---|
| Hi Cynthia, | Hello Jesse, | Mr. Purefoy: |
| Cynthia, | Dear Jesse, | Dear Mr. Purefoy: |
| Cynthia: | Dear Jesse: | |

When you are addressing a group of people, feel free to use a word such as *team* or *all*, as in "Hi team" or "Hello all."

As you exchange a few messages back and forth, take note of your associate's style. If you would feel more confident following your associate's lead, do so: imitation is a form of flattery.

Closings     For letters, the standard closing is *sincerely*. In fact, other than sincerely, most formal closings now seem passé; for example, *yours truly* and *very truly yours* sound awkward.

With e-mail, no standard protocol guides writers. Therefore, you can be more expressive with your closings.

Here are some common closings for e-mail:

| | |
|---|---|
| Take care. | Let's talk soon. |
| Hope your day goes well. | Cheers, |
| Talk to you later. | All the best, |
| Thanks for your help. | Best regards, |

Notice that the first word of each closing is capitalized, but second words are not. Since the closing *sincerely* is associated with formal business letters, reserve the use of sincerely for only the most formal e-mail message. When writing to a friend, but the relationship is somewhat formal, use *warm regards.*

Even if you use an automatic sign-off, key in your first name so that it appears above your sign-off. This may seem redundant, and it is; but closing with your first name personalizes your e-mail, which adds to a friendly tone.

## Reveal Purpose *at a Glance*

Before the reader even opens your message, you can show purpose and create a sense of urgency through your subject line.

For example, if you need the reader to take action, put the due date in the subject line, as in the following:

**Subject:** Monthly Report Due May 29
**Subject:** Action Needed on Vendor Account
**Subject:** February 11 Meeting Postponed

After you exchange information about the same topic a few times, change the subject line to reflect the evolving information. Keep the first few words of the subject line the same so that the reader can access the group of messages easily, for example:

**Subject:** February 11 Meeting Rescheduled for May 10

However, do not try to become so efficient that you put your entire message in a subject line: opening a blank message is disconcerting.

## Keep Your Message Brief

Today's world is moving at warp speed. No one has time to read lengthy messages; long messages are sometimes not even read.

Some writers are wordy because they are afraid that being too direct would be perceived as being rude; when in fact, the opposite is generally true. Readers become put off and even angry when they need to mull through long messages to understand the action that they need to take. Lost time equates to frustration.

For routine communication, start your message with purpose and action needed. (For situations when you would not craft a brief *direct message*, see pages 32-34, for *indirect* or *bad news messages*.) If you have more than one question, number your questions so that it is easier for the reader to respond to each.

Keeping your message brief is part of the editing process. Compose freely until you write the sentence that clearly states your purpose; then cut and paste it to the beginning of your message. Then begin the cutting process. Editing for brevity is not a waste of time when you realize that you are saving time for your reader, possibly enhancing the relationship.

## Do *Not* Use Text Language

Always use standard spelling, punctuation, and capitalization in business correspondence, even when you are writing to close associates. For example, if you use text abbreviations with friends at work, you may unconsciously let that habit spill over into formal communications. In addition, you never know when any message you write will be forwarded up the line of command.

Some readers cringe when they see "i" or "ur." For clarity, the personal pronoun *I* is always capitalized—in no instance is it used correctly in lower case. In addition, contractions need an apostrophe.

To reach all audiences, do not take shortcuts. The only way to communicate across cultural and generational lines is to speak in the language with which everyone is familiar. Global communication demands that standard—and most business environments are global.

## Use Visual Persuasion

Visual persuasion involves formatting a document to give readers instant access to key points. The easier it is for your reader to understand your message, the better response you will receive.

Some visual tools include bolding, italics, underscoring, and numbering. Of course, using all caps connotes shouting.

An overlooked yet critical element of visual persuasion is *white space*, which is the blank space on the page. In part, you create white space through vertical spacing: to leave one blank line, double space (DS); DS by striking *Enter* (aka *Return*) two times.

For formal documents, such as business letters, a specific amount of white space is designated between parts. However, you can improve informal documents, such as e-mail, by leaving one line of white space after your salutation and between paragraphs. Readers have an easier time understanding and responding to a message that consists of short, manageable chunks of information.

Here are some tips to make your message easily accessible:

1.  Break your message into short paragraphs.

2.  Add a line of white space (a blank line) by double spacing between parts of your message and between paragraphs.

3.  Use bullet points and numbering so that key ideas stand out.

4. Number questions so that you get a response to each one posed.

5. To stress words, use italics or bolding rather than underscoring; in electronic communication, underscoring implies hyperlink.

You will find many more guidelines for formatting in Chapter 13, *Format like a Pro*. Feel free to fast forward to that chapter before reviewing the next several chapters, which walk you step by step through principles that lead to correct, clear, concise writing.

Next, let us examine one of the only reasons why to present your message in an indirect way to your reader.

## Tailor Your Style for Your Message

Whether you are writing a letter or an e-mail, convey information using a direct approach unless you are conveying bad news.

Direct Message Style    In a direct message, put the main point in the first paragraph. For e-mail, also put the action that you need your reader to take up front; however, for letters, put action needed or next steps in the last paragraph.

Once readers understand the purpose, supporting information confirms and expands their understanding of your message. The bulk of the information follows. Give as many details as necessary, but do not stray from the principle *less is more.*

In your closing, open the door for additional communication.

Indirect or Bad News Message Style    Once in a while, everyone needs to convey news the reader does not expect or would prefer not receiving. A *bad news message* is one of the few times when you would write an indirect message rather than a direct message.

In an indirect message, include details before stating outcomes or conclusions. By explaining the logic, rationale, and background details before getting to the key point, you give the reader an opportunity to understand the *why* of the unwelcome decision.

In contrast, if you get right the point, the reader is likely to have an immediate negative reaction and may not even read the logic behind the decision.

In the introduction, state the purpose in a general way. Then give enough explanation so that the rationale leading to the news makes sense to the reader (or as much sense as possible). State your main point or bad news toward the end of the message or possibly in the conclusion.

As in the direct message, the closing paragraph of an indirect message lets your reader know that he or she may contact you or someone else for additional information.

However, take note: depending on the type of bad news you are conveying, an e-mail message or a letter is not the best choice—possibly not even a viable choice. Call or meet with the person receiving the bad news, if possible.

The most professional way to share bad news is in person; however, that is not always possible. The least desirable method is sending an e-mail message. When you must put bad news in writing, you show respect for your reader by structuring the message effectively; more precisely, convey bad news by being indirect.

The two messages that follow contain similar information. As you read each message, notice how the structure of the information affects the tone.

## Message 1: Bad News Conveyed Using *Direct Message Style*

Dear Joan:

Your request for a leave of absence has been denied.

The policy manual states that only employees who have worked with our company for a minimum of one year are eligible for a leave of absence. Even so, I checked with human resources to find out if an exception could be made for you. HR didn't think so, but they took the extra effort to contact corporate. Corporate confirmed that an exception could not be made because they receive many requests every year. If they made exceptions, the policy could be challenged legally.

I wish there were something else we could do for you. Please keep me apprised of your situation.

Best regards,

Roger

## Message 2: Bad News Conveyed Using *Indirect Message Style*

Dear Joan:

Here's information in response to your request for a leave of absence.

The policy manual states that only employees who have worked with our company for a minimum of one year are eligible for a leave of absence. Even so, I checked with human resources to find out if an exception could be made for you. HR didn't think so, but they took the extra effort to contact corporate. Corporate confirmed that an exception could not be made because they receive many requests every year. If they made exceptions, the policy could be challenged legally.

Therefore, your request for a leave of absence has been denied. I wish there were something else we could do for you. Please keep me apprised of your situation and let me know if you have more questions.

Best regards,

Roger

*Which of the two messages above has a more effective tone?*

# Avoid Micro-Messages

*Micro-messages* are the subtle, intangible messages that occur *between the lines*. Micro-messages can be either positive or negative.

When you receive a negative micro-message, you may not know how to respond.

**For example:**

- A colleague does not respond to your urgent message.
- You receive a reply but your questions are not answered.
- A client tells you about a mistake that you made and copies your supervisor.

Or maybe you are on the other side of any of the above, being the one who did not respond or answer questions fully. Without doubt, e-mail has a huge potential to destroy a person's day and even disrupt business relationships.

Let's face it, anyone can easily forget to respond to a message or overlook answering questions. How you respond to others in these situations and how they respond to you helps define the relationship. That is because business transactions are based only in part on information flow, with another part influenced by the relationship among the players.

When relationships are in good standing, a sense of trust and respect exists. However, when relationships are not in good standing, *the benefit of the doubt* ceases to exist and suspicion can begin to linger in the background of every communication. When things go wrong, the blame game begins. When this destructive dynamic takes over, business suffers.

Always remember the human elements of communication, which involve feelings and passions and fears as well as forgiveness and appreciation. No one is perfect, which means that everyone makes mistakes. By giving others leeway, they are more likely to bestow that grace upon you when you fall short.

At times, a human voice can melt barriers that written words cannot, and an apology can release the emotions of hurt feelings. Once trust is violated, relationships are challenging to mend. By working to ensure that you are not inadvertently sending a negative micro-message, you will send fewer of them. But no one is perfect.

## Apologize Gracefully

An apology is less about your mistake and more about reassuring your client that you understand the situation and want to correct it.

When a situation calls for an apology, dissolve hurt feelings by apologizing quickly and humbly. Keep your apology simple: as Henry David Thoreau once advised, "One cannot too soon forget his errors and misdemeanors; for to dwell on them is to add to the offense."

Also, take the opportunity to reinforce the relationship by showing your client appreciation.

**Don't say**    I'm really sorry that you feel slighted I couldn't call sooner, but I was so busy and had a thousand people pulling me from different directions. Your call was on my priority list, but I couldn't get to it until now.

**Do Say:**    I apologize for not getting back to you sooner; thank you for being patient. I appreciate the opportunity to work with you. What can I do now to assist you?

If you feel emotional, your words will convey your feelings as well as your ideas. When someone writes you with emotion, try to understand what provoked the person's actions; then wait until you gain a clear perspective *before* you respond.

To some extent, communication mishaps are inevitable. The sooner you apologize in a simple yet authentic way, the sooner you will once again dance in step with your client.

## Ask Questions to Get a Response

At times, writers pose vague comments, thinking that being too direct may sound rude. However, readers do not always understand how to respond to vague comments or even necessarily realize that the writer expects a response.

For example, as you read the two sentences below, notice which one makes it easier for you to give a response:

**Comment:**    When you get a chance, please let me know your availability for a meeting next week.

**Question:**    Would you be available to meet with me next week? If so, what day works best for you?

When writers pose a direct question, their readers find it almost difficult *not* to respond.

For the most part, being direct is a communication style that shows respect to the reader because it clarifies what the writer expects. Here are two more examples:

**Comment:**    I'd like to know more about the Jones proposal.
**Question:**    What can you tell me about the Jones proposal?

**Comment:**    I'll be attending the upcoming conference in Boston and would be interested in discussing our project.

**Question:**    I'll be attending the upcoming conference in Boston. Would you have time to meet with me to discuss our project? If so, would you have time on Tuesday?

When you edit, clarify the difference between vague comments and questions, identifying the kind of response you need. As you incorporate more questions into your messages, notice if you get a higher ratio of responses.

## Recap

By taking a conservative approach in the way that you structure a message, you reach a broad audience; you also avoid sending micro-messages of which you might not even be aware.

By following the guidelines presented here, you are following best practices, molding your message so that it gets the best results.

## Action Steps

What are your *takeaways*? What key points do you plan to apply?

-----

-----

-----

-----

# 4

# Control the Core

Good editing produces good writing. The most powerful unit of editing is the sentence, and the most powerful element of the sentence is its core: *the verb and its subject.*

The **sentence core** is also the most significant unit in grammar because together the subject and verb create meaning:

Marcy arrived.
Bill left.
Mary wept.

The hub or focal point of every sentence is its verb, and the verb determines the subject and the object, if there is one.

The best way to identify the **grammatical subject** (which is what most people commonly think of as the subject) is to identify the verb first and then work backward in the sentence. That is because in English, the grammatical subject almost always precedes the verb.

However, there are two types of subjects: a grammatical subject and a **real subject**, which drives the action of the verb. Though all sentences have a grammatical subject, not all sentences have a real subject, which may come as a surprise.

In brief, a sentence core is strong when its grammatical subject and real subject are the same. (You learn more about real subjects in this chapter and Chapter 6, *Keep Verbs Alive and Active*, which discusses active and passive voice.)

When the sentence core is strong, the *subject and verb* give you a glimpse into the meaning of the sentence.

Let us look at how structure can lead to dynamic writing.

## Dynamic Sentences

Effectively written sentences come alive to the reader, provoking understanding, insight, and even action. Thus, when you think of sentence structure, stop thinking about your elementary education experience. Instead, open yourself to the exciting possibilities that become real once you can control structure to bring your readers to a higher level of meaning and action.

*A **sentence** consists of a verb and its subject and expresses a complete thought.* In English, neither readers nor speakers find much meaning until hearing both the subject and the verb of a sentence. In the following examples, the subject and verb are in bold.

**Example 1:**

**George Clooney**, who is a talented sales representative on the East Coast in the Boston area and who has been recently promoted to district manager because of his astute marketing skills, **will speak** at our next regional meeting.

Was the above engaging and easy to follow? Of course not, but *why not?*

First, consider the amount of intervening information between the main verb, *will speak*, and its subject, *George Clooney*. Also consider the minor clauses (who clauses) within the main clause.

Though reading the above example may not have been pleasant, that is the point. When readers have difficulty understanding, they lose interest quickly. Let's see how to revise the above example so that the reader more easily connects to it.

**Example 2:**

**George Clooney will speak** at our next regional meeting. **George is** our sales representative in Boston, and **he has** recently **been promoted** to district manager because of his astute marketing skills.

In Example 2, the subject and verb are close to each other and close to the beginning of the sentence. In fact, the information is broken into three main clauses, each with its subject and verb close to each other and close to the beginning of the sentence.

Notice that Example 2 did not contain the phrase "on the East Coast." Boston is obviously on the East Coast. Once you focus on the sentence core, information that adds no value for the reader begins to stand out. (Chapter 8, *Be Concise*, gives insight into which types of information to cut.)

One way to vary sentences from this simple subject – verb – object pattern without diluting the sentence core is to begin with an introductory phrase or clause. The key point here is that *subjects and verbs belong together*.

Another difference between the two examples above is sentence length. Example 1 above contains 38 words, while Example 2 breaks the information into two shorter sentences, with the longer sentence containing 22 words.

Let's take a look at how sentence length affects readability.

## Sentence Length

Have you ever had to re-read a sentence because it was difficult to understand? If so, was it an unusually long sentence? Though there is no exact prescription for how long a sentence should be, the average reader finds it difficult to retain information when sentences become unusually long. Here is an editing tip that you can apply at once to improve your writing:

*Limit your sentences to 25 words or fewer.*

**For example**:

When writers include too much information in a sentence, readers tend to become confused and frustrated because, by the time that they get to the end of a long sentence, many readers have already forgotten what the beginning of the sentence was about and need to go back to the beginning and reread it again, especially if the writer uses complicated words and an abstract voice. (66 words)

If you become irritated when you read long sentences, realize that your readers do too. In addition, when sentences are long, writing decisions are more difficult.

Writing shorter sentences gives you more control and makes editing easier: the shorter the sentence, the less complicated the grammar and punctuation. Simple, clear, and concise writing is reader-friendly writing. So use the following as your guideline:

*Less is more.*

When you write long, complicated sentences, count the number of words. You may be shocked to find that you currently write sentences that are 40, 50, and even 60 or more words in length. If cutting words is not enough to bring the word count to 25 (or close to it), break the information into shorter sentences. At times, you will need to do both.

Limiting sentence length forces you to be more concise, as does controlling the sentence core; so let's look at how to write effective sentences using real subjects and strong verbs.

## Real Subjects and Strong Verbs

Together the subject and verb form the sentence core, and the sentence core is the focal point at which grammar and writing style cross paths.

The most effective type of sentence core consists of a real subject that drives the action of a strong verb. For example, starting a sentence with *it* or *there* ensures that your sentence will not have a strong sentence core (as shown in italics below):

**Weak:** *There are* many unresolved decisions.
**Revised:** Many *decisions remain* unresolved.

**Weak:** *It is* time to start the meeting.
**Revised:** The *meeting starts* now.

**Weak:** *It is* an important decision.
**Revised:** This *decision determines* our future.

**Weak:** *It is* time for change.
**Revised:** The *time* for change *is* now.

Of course, at times a writer must start a sentence with *it* or *there*. In fact, one of the most memorable sentences in literature starts with *it*:

"It was the best of times, it was the worst of times . . . ." (*A Tale of Two Cities*, Charles Dickens, 1859)

Writers who know the rules can effectively break the rules to create exciting prose. For example, do you remember the opening phrase to the original Star Trek series: "To *boldly* go where no man has gone before"? The writer purposely created a split infinitive by stating "to *boldly* go" rather than "to go *boldly*," which does not quite have the same zing.

The "no split infinitive rule" was fabricated centuries back by grammarians who were also Latin scholars. Applying the rules of Latin to English doesn't exactly work. In Latin, one-word infinitives cannot be split: *dare, facere, vincere*, and so on. Even so, avoid splitting an infinitive unless you split it on purpose.

Creative writers break rules for effect more often than business writers do. However, regardless of the type of writing, know the rules *before* you break them, or you are likely to be making a mistake rather than a decision.

When you read the subject and verb of a sentence aloud, you can tell immediately if you have an effective core. In addition, once you pair a strong verb with a real subject, much of your editing falls naturally into place. You immediately see which words to cut, and your sentence practically writes itself.

Let's look at how to control the sentence core and be more concise by getting rid of redundant subjects.

## Redundant Subjects

A *compound subject* consists or two or more words or phrases.

**For example**:     *Carol* and *Joyce* attended the reunion.

                      My *laptop* and *cell phone* are on the desk.

Though compound subjects can offer new meaning, be on the lookout for those that are redundant.

**Weak:**       My *thoughts* and *ideas* about the topic are clear.

The *issues* and *concerns* were discussed at the last meeting.

**Revised:**       My *thoughts* about the topic are clear.

The *issues* were discussed at the last meeting.

Next, let's look at compound verbs.

## Redundant Verbs

A *compound verb* consists of two or more main verbs along with their helpers. However, just as subjects can be redundant at times, so can verbs.

**Weak:**       My associate *had called* and *asked* me for a favor.

I *read* and *analyzed* the report.

The assistant *listened* to responses and *recorded* them.

**Revised:**       My associate *asked* me for a favor.

I *analyzed* the report.

The assistant *recorded* their responses.

When you use compound verbs, be sure that each verb offers new and relevant information. To review more about redundancy, fast-forward to *Chapter 8, Be Concise.*

Next, let's look at how conjunctions play a role in sentence structure and style.

# Conjunctions

Right now, you may think conjunctions are unimportant because they are not nearly as exciting as other parts of speech, such as verbs and adjectives. However, conjunctions pull the reader's thinking along with the meaning you are trying to convey. By affecting the quality and flow of a sentence, conjunctions play an important role in writing style.

Conjunctions also play a major role in determining where to place commas and semicolons, which you review in the next chapter. By spending a few minutes memorizing each category of conjunction along with a few examples of each, you will have a much easier time understanding punctuation.

The three types of conjunctions that play a major role in style and grammar are **coordinating, subordinating**, and **adverbial**.

1. *Coordinating conjunctions* connect equal grammatical parts. There are seven coordinating conjunctions, and they are *and, but, or, for, nor, so,* and *yet*. Together they form the acronym *FANBOYS.*

2. *Subordinating conjunctions* show relationships between ideas and, in the process, make one idea dependent on the other; subordinating conjunctions appear as single words or short phrases: *after, although, as soon as, because, before, even though, if, since, until, when, whereas, while,* among others.

3. *Adverbial conjunctions* build bridges between ideas, pulling your reader's thinking along with your intent. Adverbial conjunctions are easy to identify; here are a few: *however, therefore, thus, hence, for example, in conclusion,* and so on.

Though writing generally does not flow well when it consists of short, choppy sentences, sometimes these types of sentences create a desired dramatic effect.

**For example**:     Conan arrived late today. He resigned.

However, for the most part, choppy writing is not effective.

**Choppy**:     Jay sold his condo. He needs to relocate.

To reduce the choppy effect, connect the two sentences by using a subordinate or an adverbial conjunction. In the revisions below, each sentence uses a transitional word to bridge the cause and effect, aiding readers in drawing a connection between the two clauses.

**Revised**:     Jay sold his condo *since* he needs to relocate.
     Jay sold his condo *because* he needs to relocate.
     Jay sold his condo; *unfortunately*, he needs to relocate.

Conjunctions also play a role in creating a reader-friendly writing style because they cue the reader to the meaning you are conveying. For example, the word *however* signals the reader that the next idea will contrast with the preceding one; *therefore* points to a conclusion; and the phrase *in conclusion* sends the message, "Yay! The end is near."

Readers appreciate these kinds of cues, which you can also provide by adjusting information flow.

## Information Flow

Information flow is about ordering information so that meaning flows logically. To start, let's break information into two broad categories: *familiar* ideas and *unfamiliar* ideas.[1]

1. Think of familiar information as *old information,* which tends to be more global than specific.
2. Think of unfamiliar ideas as *new information*, which tends to be more specific than global.

When a sentence starts with a familiar idea, readers have an easier time making a connection to the new idea. (In the examples below, old information is shown in italics.)

**New to *Old*:**   Changes in consumer spending habits during the economic downturn will be *the topic of our next report.*

When you edit, switch the order so that the sentence begins with the familiar or old information, which is "the topic of our next report" or simply, "in our next report," for example:

**Òld to New:**   *In our next report,* we will discuss changes in consumer spending habits during the economic downturn.

By beginning the sentence with the familiar, you provide an anchor for your readers and ease them into the unfamiliar information.

Here is another example in which "our first team meeting" is the familiar or old information:

**New to *Old*:**   A set of ground rules and a membership survey about recent policy changes need to be developed *at our first team meeting*.

***Old* to New:**   *At our first team meeting*, we need to develop a set of ground rules and a membership survey about recent policy changes.

When you compose, you may find that it feels natural to put new information at the beginning of a sentence. That is partly because the new information is foremost on your mind. When you edit, revise the information flow for your reader.

In fact, information at the end of a sentence generally stands out more for a reader than information at the beginning or middle: the subject and verb set the stage for information at the end of a sentence to be meaningful. The official term is *end stress*. Thus, when you put information at the end of a sentence, you are delegating it to the most important position.

All sentences are not equal and do not merit the same amount of fine-tuned editing. Therefore, apply the principle of end stress when you are crafting especially important sentences.

In addition to old and new information, you will encounter a third category of information: *empty information.*

*Empty information* is redundant or irrelevant information.

A sentence that contains all old information is empty. Even relevant information becomes irrelevant, and possibly confusing, when repeated. Therefore, when you write two sentences that say the same thing, cut one of them. Cutting is the most painful part of editing.

# Recap

To write reader-friendly sentences, focus on the sentence core and information flow. To develop a strong core, use a real subject that drives a strong verb. Limit sentence length to about 25 words or fewer. Follow old to new information flow to develop reader-friendly sentences, and cut empty information.

As well as helping to determine where to place commas and semicolons, conjunctions also play a role in creating an effective writing style. Think of conjunctions as comma signals.

1. *Coordinating conjunctions*, such as *and, but, or, nor, for, so*, and *yet*, connect equal grammatical parts.

2. *Subordinating conjunctions*, such as *before, after*, and *although*, cue the reader to how ideas are related.

3. *Adverbial conjunctions*, such as *however* and *therefore*, bridge ideas and function as transition words; they also pull the reader's thinking along with your intention.

# Action Steps

What are your *takeaways*? What key points do you plan to apply?

## Reference

1. Joseph M. Williams, *Style: Toward Clarity and Grace*, The University of Chicago Press, 1990, pages 52-57.

# 5

# Don't *Pause* for Commas

Have you ever read a sentence over and again looking for the *right pause* and placing a comma (or even a semicolon) in a different place each time?

Part of the problem is that identifying pauses works at times. You see, grammar creates natural breaks; and at *some* of these breaks, a comma would be needed. However, are you confident about whether to place a comma, a semicolon, or a period at the break? In fact, are you sure when you pause that you are pausing at a grammatical break?

Unless you know how to identify natural breaks in grammar, rely on comma rules instead of pauses. In fact, comma rules also teach you structure, giving you a foundation for understanding core grammar and editing principles. In general, here are two guidelines to apply:

1.  Use a comma to introduce, set off, or separate elements within a sentence.
2.  Use a semicolon in place of a period to separate independent clauses (in other words, to separate complete sentences).

Let's work on commas first and then glance at semicolons as well as colons, dashes, and ellipses.

Each of the 12 basic comma rules includes an abbreviation, which is shown in parentheses; for example, Rule 2: Comma Conjunction (CONJ). Use the abbreviation as a proofreading mark as you edit.

## Basic Comma Rules

### Rule 1: The Sentence Core Rules (SCR)
*Do not separate a subject and verb with only one comma.*

### Rule 2: Comma Conjunction (CONJ)
*Use a comma to separate two independent clauses when they are joined by a coordinating conjunction* (and, but, or, nor, for, so, yet).

### Rule 3: Comma Series (SER)
*Use a comma to separate three or more items in a series.*

### Rule 4: Comma Introductory (INTRO)
*Place a comma after a word, phrase, or dependent clause that introduces an independent clause.*

### Rule 5: Comma Nonrestrictive (NR)
*Use commas to set off nonessential (nonrestrictive) elements.*

### Rule 6: Comma Parenthetical (PAR)
*Use commas to set off a word or phrase that interrupts the flow of a sentence.*

### Rule 7: Comma Direct Address (DA)
*Use commas to set off the name or title of a person addressed directly.*

### Rule 8: Comma Appositive (AP)
*Use commas to set off the restatement of a noun or pronoun.*

### Rule 9: Comma Addresses and Dates (AD)

*Use commas to set off the parts of addresses and dates.*

### Rule 10: Comma Words Omitted (WO)

*Use a comma for the omission of a word or words that play a structural role in sentences.*

### Rule 11: Comma Direct Quotation (DQ)

*Use commas to set off a direct quotation within a sentence.*

### Rule 12: Comma Contrasting Expression or Afterthought (CEA)

*Use a comma to separate a contrasting expression or an afterthought.*

Punctuation speaks to your readers in subtle ways and contributes to clear understanding.

You will find more details along with practice exercises and keys in *A Guide for Business Writing* as well as at the book's Web site, www.youngcommunication.com (click on *Learning Activities* tab).

## Comma Rules

Here is a brief explanation along with examples of each comma rule.

### Rule 1: The Sentence Core Rules (SCR)

*Do not separate a subject and verb with only one comma.*

As you know, the sentence core is the most powerful element of any sentence. Placing one comma between a subject and its verb creates a major grammatical error.

However, setting off information between a subject and verb with a *pair of commas* is acceptable (for example, see Rule 5: Comma Nonrestrictive).

## Rule 2: Comma Conjunction (CONJ)

*Use a comma to separate two independent clauses when they are joined by a coordinating conjunction* (and, but, or, nor, for, so, yet).

In the following examples, coordinating conjunctions are shown in italics.

**For example:**     Bill stayed late, *and* he worked on the proposal.

Marie left the book, *but* George did not pick it up.

Be careful not to add a comma before a coordinating conjunction when only the second part of a compound verb follows it, for example:

**Incorrect:**     Bob completed the proposal, *and* sent it to John.

**Corrected:**     Bob completed the proposal *and* sent it to John.

When a comma is not used to separate two independent clauses that are joined by a coordinating conjunction, the result is a run-on sentence. In the following, the subjects, verbs, and conjunctions are shown in italics.

**Incorrect:**     The *project was* successful *so we plan* to start next week.

**Corrected:**     The *project was* successful**,** *so we plan* to start next week.

*Note: So that* is a subordinating conjunction and would not be preceded by a comma.

# Rule 3: Comma Series (SER)

*Use a comma to separate three or more items in a series.*

**For example:**     Please prepare *potatoes, peas,* and *carrots.*

Lee enjoys *walking, doing yoga,* and *swimming.*

The estate was left to *Bob, Rose, Bill, and Marie.*

You may have learned that the comma before the conjunction *and* in a series is not required. That is true. Although the comma before *and* is not required, the comma is preferred. To see why, consider the following:

1.  In the first example above, would you prepare the "potatoes, peas, and carrots" separately or mixed?
2.  If the comma were missing after *peas,* as in "potatoes, peas and carrots," would you prepare the peas and carrots separately or mixed?
3.  In the third example, would the estate necessarily be split the same way if the comma after *Bill* were missing?

**For example:**     The estate was left to *Bob, Rose, Bill* and *Marie.*

In fact, the above sentence is open for debate. Some could argue that the estate should be split only three ways, with Bill and Marie sharing a third. And, unfortunately, a court of law has been known to agree, with "Bill" and "Marie" being left only one-sixth each instead of one-fourth each.

For clarity, separate each entity (or individual) with a comma so that a debate does not ensue, especially in legal documents such as wills and trusts.

At times, writers mistakenly separate only two items with a comma. This mistake is common when the items are long phrases, such as the ones shown in italics in the examples below:

**Incorrect:**     The assistant provided *a series of excellent examples that sparked debate*, and *a good recap of the issues discussed at the meeting*.

**Corrected:**     The assistant provided *a series of excellent examples that sparked debate* and *a good recap of the issues discussed at the meeting*.

The next rule, comma introductory, involves using subordinating and adverbial conjunctions. (To review conjunctions, see pages 25 to 27.)

## Rule 4: Comma Introductory (INTRO)

*Place a comma after a word, phrase, or dependent clause that introduces an independent clause.*

Since this rule is a bit complicated, let us break it down into the various parts: word, phrase, and dependent clause.

**Introductory Word**     In general, *word* refers to an adverbial conjunction such as *therefore*, *however*, and *consequently*, for example:

*However*, I was not able to attend the conference.
*Therefore*, we will meet in Boston this year.

**Introductory Phrase**    In general, *phrase* refers to a gerund, infinitive, or prepositional phrase, for example:

> *Leaving the airport*, I took a taxi into the city. (gerund phrase)
> *To arrive earlier*, Mitchell changed his schedule. (infinitive phrase)
> *During the meeting*, he spoke about the plan. (prepositional phrase)

**Introductory (Dependent) Clause**    Dependent clauses begin with a subordinating conjunction, such as *although, because, if, since* and *while*, for example:

> *Although* I am busy, we can meet this Friday morning.
> *Before* you arrive, (you) call my assistant.
> *Unless* I am late, you will not hear from me.

Sometimes writers mistakenly place a comma after a subordinating conjunction, for example:

**Incorrect:**    *Although*, the information is timely, we cannot use it.
**Corrected:**    *Although* the information is timely, we cannot use it.

Place the comma after the dependent clause, not directly after the subordinating conjunction. In other words, whenever a writer places a comma after a subordinating conjunction, the comma is most likely a mistake.

## Rule 5: Comma Nonrestrictive (NR)

*Use commas to set off nonessential (nonrestrictive) elements.*

Though nonessential elements (or explanations) add value, a sentence does not need them to be clear and complete. When nonessential information is taken out of a sentence, the sentence will still make sense.

*A word of caution*: This rule pertains primarily to *who* and *which* clauses that are not essential for clarity; do not set off prepositional phrases with commas.

Read the following examples that illustrate this rule (*who* clauses are shown in italics):

**Clear:**     Alice Walker, *who is a prestigious author,* will be the keynote speaker.

**Clear:**     Alice Walker will be the keynote speaker.

In the example above, you would still know who the keynote speaker would be even if the *who* clause were removed. Now read the example below, which contains a restrictive clause:

**Clear:**     The woman *who is a prestigious author* will be the keynote speaker.

**Unclear:**   The woman will be the keynote speaker. *Which woman?*

The key to understanding this rule lies in the difference between the meaning of the words **restrictive** and **nonrestrictive**.

1. *Restrictive information* is essential and should not be set off with commas.
2. *Nonrestrictive information* is not essential and can be set off with commas.

*Note: Which clauses* tend to be nonrestrictive, whereas *that clauses* are restrictive.

The next few comma rules also relate to setting off nonrestrictive information with commas.

## Rule 6: Comma Parenthetical (PAR)

*Use commas to set off a word or phrase that interrupts the flow of a sentence.*

This rule applies to adverbial conjunctions or other short phrases interjected into a sentence. By interrupting the flow of the sentence, a parenthetical expression places stress on the words immediately preceding it or following it. Because these elements are nonessential to the meaning and clarity of a sentence, use commas to set them off.

The three sentences below contain parenthetical expressions, which are in italics and set off with commas.

**For example:**      Mr. Connors did not, *however,* attend the ceremony.

You can, *therefore*, place your order after 5 p.m.

The project, *in my opinion*, needs improvement.

A common mistake occurs when a writer uses a semicolon in place of one of the commas, for example:

**Incorrect:**      Ms. Willis; *in fact*, approved the request today.

**Corrected:**      Ms. Willis, *in fact*, approved the request today.

Though a semicolon can precede an adverbial conjunction, that construction involves two sentences. In those cases, the adverbial conjunction functions as a bridge or a transition rather than an interrupter. (The next section in this chapter reviews semicolons.)

Another common mistake occurs when a writer uses only one comma before or after an adverbial conjunction rather than a set of commas, for example:

**Incorrect:**       Mr. Jones, *however* will plan this year's event.

**Corrected:**    Mr. Jones, *however*, will plan this year's event.

In addition to using *however* as an adverbial conjunction, you can also use it as an adverb. When using however as an adverb, do not set it off with commas, as in the following:

> We will do the project *however* you prefer.

Though adverbial conjunctions are usually nonessential elements in terms of sentence structure, these conjunctions play an important role in writing style. Adverbial conjunctions give vital clues to meaning, helping your reader identify key points.

## Rule 7: Comma Direct Address (DA)

*Use commas to set off the name or title of a person addressed directly.*

A direct address can appear anywhere in a sentence: at the beginning, middle, or end, as shown below in italics.

**For example:**    *Donald*, you can arrange the meeting in Dallas.

                      I invited everyone in the department, *Marge*.

                      Your instructions, *Professor*, were clear and concise.

In each of the above examples, notice that the direct address is not the subject of the sentence. Each of the following sentences also contains a direct address (shown in italics), but the subject of each sentence is *implied*. As you read each sentence, ask yourself, "Who is performing the action of the verb?"

**For example:**   Thank you, *Astrid*, for speaking on my behalf.

Feel free to contact me when you are in town, *David*.

*Traci*, please assist me with the spring conference.

In the first sentence above, the implied subject is *I understood* (I); in the second and third, it is *you understood* (you):

(I) thank you, Astrid, for speaking on my behalf.

(You) feel free to contact me when you are in town, David.

Traci, (you) please assist me with the spring conference.

In sentences that contain a direct address, the subject is often implied.

## Rule 8: Comma Appositive (AP)

*Use commas to set off the restatement of a noun or pronoun.*

With an appositive, an equivalency exists between the noun and its descriptor. In the examples below, appositives are shown in italics.

**For example:**   Helen, *my cousin*, requested the date.

Mr. Frank, *the building manager*, let us in.

Check to see if a descriptor is an appositive by asking questions such as the following:

Who is Helen? *My cousin*

Who is my cousin? *Helen*

Who is Mr. Frank? *The building manager*

Who is the building manager? *Mr. Frank*

When a writer uses only one comma before or after an appositive, it creates a mistake and changes the meaning of the sentence, for example:

**Incorrect:**        Josef, my former boss gave me the information.

**Corrected:**        Josef, my former boss, gave me the information.

In the incorrect version, "Josef" becomes a direct address, which means that Josef is being spoken to rather than being spoken about.

Appositives can be restrictive as well as nonrestrictive. A *restrictive appositive* is essential for clear meaning and would not be set off with commas.

For example, let us say that you have a client named Charles who is joining you and a friend for dinner.

**Appositive:**        My client, Charles, will join us for dinner.

Surrounding information with commas implies that the information between the commas could be removed and the sentence would still be correct and clear in meaning. Therefore, the above sentence translates to "My client will join us for dinner."

If Charles were your only client, the sentence would still be clear in meaning. However, since you are likely to have more than one client, taking "Charles" out of the sentence makes the meaning unclear: which client will join you for dinner?

**Restrictive Appositive:**        My client Charles will join us for dinner.

**Restrictive Appositives:**        Two of my friends are in the lobby. My friend Jean is wearing green, and my friend Eileen is wearing blue.

However, be on the lookout for nonrestrictive appositives, which are far more common than restrictive appositives.

## Rule 9: Comma Addresses and Dates (AD)

*Use commas to set off the parts of addresses and dates.*

Writers make many mistakes with this rule, especially when an address or date occurs in the middle of a sentence.

In the following examples, notice how commas surround *Illinois* and *California* as well as *Italy* and *August 15*:

**For example:**    Phoenix, Arizona, is the best city for the summit.

Jane has worked in Chicago, Illinois, for five years.

We will meet on Sunday, August 15, in Rome, Italy, to celebrate the *Ferragosta*.

Does it surprise you to learn that a comma is required after the state name when a city and state occur in the middle of a sentence? If so, you are not alone; the following mistake is common:

**Incorrect:**    Dallas, Texas is a great city to start a business.
**Corrected:**    Dallas, Texas, is a great city to start a business.

When a complete date occurs within a sentence, use commas to set off the month, day, and year:

**Incorrect:**    Rose listed May 29, 2010 as her start date.
**Corrected:**    Rose listed May 29, 2010, as her start date.

However, a *serious error* occurs when a comma is placed between the month and the day, for example:

**Incorrect:**     May, 29, 2010 was the date on the application.

**Corrected:**     May 29, 2010, was the date on the application.

When only a month and year appear together, a comma is not needed, for example:

The June 2013 report was published late.

Comma addresses and dates (AD) is a form of comma nonrestrictive, similar to the other comma rules in which information is set off.


## Rule 10: Comma Words Omitted (WO)

*Use a comma for the omission of a word or words that play a structural role in sentences.*

Comma words omitted (WO) does not occur frequently; oftentimes, the word that has been omitted is *that* or *and*.

**For example:**     The problem is *that* the current situation looks grim.
The problem is, the current situation looks grim.

Mr. Adams presented the long and boring report.
Mr. Adams presented the long, boring report.

Most of the time when the word *that* is removed, the flow of the sentence is not affected and a comma would not be needed.

# Rule 11: Comma Direct Quotation (DQ)

*Use commas to set off a direct quotation within a sentence.*

Set off a person's exact words with quotation marks and commas; however, do not set off an indirect quotation because it is not a speaker's exact words.

**Direct Quotation:** Gabrielle said, "I have an appointment," and then she left abruptly.

**Indirect Quotation:** Gabrielle said that she had an appointment, and then she left abruptly.

Short quotations built into the flow of a sentence do not need to be set off with commas.

**Short Quotations:** The advice "Give the project your best this time" sounded patronizing, not encouraging.

In direct quotations, capitalize the first word, as shown above.

Some confusion exists about the placement of commas and periods with quotation marks—in part, that's because punctuation styles vary from country to country. In the United States, **closed punctuation style** is standard. Here are rules for using quotation marks in **closed punctuation style**:

1. For commas and periods, place quotation marks on the outside.
2. For semicolons and colons, place quotation marks on the inside.
3. For exclamation points and question marks, place quotation marks based on meaning, either on the outside or inside.

*Note:* The British use **open punctuation style.** So when in Great Britain, feel free to place quotation marks on the inside of commas and periods.

### Rule 12: Comma Contrasting Expression or Afterthought (CEA)

*Use a comma to separate a contrasting expression or an afterthought.*

A contrasting expression or an afterthought catches the reader's attention, adding an interesting twist to writing style by creating a conversational flow.

**For example:**    Go ahead and put the property on the market, if possible.

I asked for the information to process the sale, not lose it.

Now let's review semicolons, a punctuation mark that many business writers avoid because they fear using it incorrectly. However, not using a semicolon where one is needed often results in a run-on sentence.

## Semicolon Rules

Have you ever heard of the saying, "semicolon in place of period"? Most of the time, you would be using a semicolon correctly if you could substitute a period for it.

### Rule 1: Semicolon No Conjunction (NC)

*Use a semicolon to separate two independent clauses that are joined without a conjunction.*

In other words, when not using a conjunction between clauses, use a semicolon (or a period) to separate the independent clauses.

This semicolon rule relates closely to comma conjunction (CONJ).

**For example:**
>Al went to the store, *but* he forgot to buy bread. (CONJ)
>Al went to the store; he forgot to buy bread. (NC)
>Al went to the store. He forgot to buy bread. (period)

Notice how each sentence has a slightly different effect based on its punctuation. In the example above that uses a period, do you see how choppy the writing sounds, thereby breaking up the sentences?

Apply the semicolon no conjunction (NC) rule when two sentences are closely related, especially when one or both sentences are short.

## Rule 2: Semicolon Transition (TRANS)
*Place a semicolon before and a comma after an adverbial conjunction that acts as a transition between two independent clauses.*

As a review, common adverbial conjunctions are *however, therefore,* and *consequently.*

Semicolon transition corresponds to comma parenthetical. When an adverbial conjunction interrupts one independent clause, it is a parenthetical expression; set it off with commas.

**For example:**     Bob, *however*, will determine the fees. (PAR)

When an adverbial conjunction functions as a bridge between two independent clauses, the semicolon transition rule applies.

**For example:**     Bob will determine the fees; *however*, he is open to suggestions. (TRANS)

If you avoided semicolons prior to learning the rules, you may have put a comma (instead of the needed semicolon) after the first clause, for example:

**Incorrect:** Bob will determine the fees, *however*, he is open to suggestions.

The above example is a run-on sentence, which occurs when a writer uses a comma where a semicolon (or period) would belong. A run-on sentence is a serious grammatical error.

Here are a few more examples of the semicolon transition rule (TRANS) with adverbial conjunctions shown in italics:

**For example:**

Lidia wrote the grant; *therefore*, she should be on the committee.

The grant was accepted; *as a result*, we will receive funding.

You should call their office; *however*, (you) wait an hour.

Now that you have reviewed this rule, can you see how you may have needed to use a semicolon instead of a comma at times?

## Rule 3: Semicolon Because of Conjunction (BC)

*When a clause needs major and minor separations, use semicolons for major breaks and commas for minor breaks.*

This semicolon rule differs from the other two rules because it does not involve a full stop; in other words, this rule does not follow the *semicolon in place of period* rule of thumb that you learned earlier.

One time to apply this rule would be when listing a series of city and state names:

**Semicolon BC:** Joni will travel to Dallas, Texas; Buffalo, New York; and Boston, Massachusetts.

Since the state names need commas around them, reading the previous sentence *without* semicolons would be confusing:

**Incorrect:**         Joni will travel to Dallas, Texas, Buffalo, New York, and Boston, Massachusetts.

Also apply this rule when listing a series of names and titles:

**Semicolon BC:**      The committee members are Jeremy Smith, director of finance; Marjorie Lou Kirk, assistant vice president; Carson Michaels, accountant; and Malory Willowbrook, broker.

A more complicated example would include major and minor clauses within a sentence:

**Semicolon BC:**      Millicent asked for a raise; and since she was a new employee, I deferred to Jackson's opinion.

**Semicolon BC:**      Dr. Jones suggested the procedure; but I was unable to help, so he asked Dr. Bender.

The semicolon because of comma (BC) rule occurs less frequently than the other types of semicolons; that is because most sentences do not call for both major and minor breaks. Even though you will not use this semicolon rule as often as the others, this rule is nonetheless necessary at times.

Next, let us look at the colon, a versatile and commanding mark of punctuation.

# The Colon

In general, the colon is a strong mark of punctuation that alerts the reader to information that will be illustrated.

Here are two common uses of the colon:

1. After salutations of business letters (and formal e-mail messages), for example: *Dear Mr. Jones:*
2. At the end of one sentence when the following sentence illustrates it, for example: *Friday was a great day: the CEO approved my promotion.*

*Note:* At times, writers mistakenly use a semicolon (rather than a colon) after a salutation (as in "Dear Mr. Jones;"). *A **semicolon** would never be used after a salutation.*

# The Dash

The dash is the most versatile mark of punctuation, at times replacing the comma, the semicolon, the period, and even the colon. The dash adds energy, making information stand out.

Though you can use the dash in formal documents, you will most often find the dash used in informal communications. Also, do not overuse the dash or your writing will sound choppy.

**For example:**
Bob called on Friday—he said that he'd arrive by noon today.
Thank you for your help—the package arrived on time.

Though the dash is different from the hyphen, use hyphens to create a dash.

1. Create an *em* dash by using two hyphens without a space before, between, or after them (as shown above).
2. Create an *en* dash by using two hyphens, but this time place a space before and after the hyphens. (Thank you – the package arrived on time.)

Though an *en* dash is now acceptable for some types of writing, an *em* dash is the traditional choice.

Once again, overusing dashes is similar to overusing colons or exclamation points. Writers enjoy using them, but readers tire of them; so use them sparingly. However, if you have never used a dash in your writing, try it. Dashes add energy and are fun to use.

## The Ellipses

*Ellipses* is plural for *ellipsis marks*. Ellipses indicate that information is missing, thereby removing an otherwise awkward gap.

In formal documents, ellipses allow writers to adapt quotations by leaving out less relevant information, making the main idea stand out. In informal documents, ellipses allow writers to jump from one idea to another without completing their thoughts. Ellipses also allow writers to convey a sense of uncertainty without coming right out and stating it.

Ellipsis marks consist of three periods with one space before, between, and after each period (or "dot").

**For example**:
This doesn't make sense to me . . . let me know what you think.

Some software programs create ellipses when you space once, type three periods in a row, and then space once again; but this style is less traditional and not recommended for formal documents.

As with dashes, use ellipsis marks sparingly, even for informal use. For formal or informal use, display ellipsis marks correctly.

## Writing Style: Punctuation and Flow

Experiment with punctuation. Notice how the rhythm and tone of each sentence below changes based on the way it is punctuated:

Johnnie offered Jay the job: he wants to retire.
Johnnie offered Jay the job—he wants to retire.
Johnnie offered Jay the job . . . he wants to retire.

Punctuation is one more tool to help you connect with your reader and get your message across, helping you express your voice.

## Recap

Correct punctuation adds credibility to writing. Along with commas, use the semicolon, the colon, the dash, and the ellipses to add variety and flair to your writing. Emphasize information by using a dash, and use ellipses to fill gaps or express uncertainty. However, use dashes and ellipses sparingly.

## Action Steps

What are your *takeaways*? What key points do you plan to apply?

# 6

# Keep Verbs Alive and Active

If your dominant voice is passive, shifting to active voice is the most powerful change you can make to improve your writing style and your results.

Active voice is clear and direct because the subject and verb are doing their prescribed jobs. In contrast, passive voice complicates meaning because the subject does not drive the verb, and the verb does not create action.

Writers can also take the life out of a verb by turning it into a noun. The process is called *nominalization*. Combine nominalized verbs with passive voice and, well, writing becomes unnecessarily complicated. In today's world, complicated writing is a time vampire: the world now demands clear, concise, active writing.

Passive voice, however, does have a legitimate and necessary place in writing when used with purpose. For example, passive voice is the tactful voice: use passive voice to avoid pointing blame. As well, use passive in academic and scientific writing—but even those arenas are taking a stand to increase the use of active voice.

Most business writers, however, use passive voice out of habit. In fact, some may argue that meaning changes when they revise passive text to active voice. Though meaning does not change, the message is more direct, and thus the tone may change.

Passive voice is the tactful voice because the *real subject* (the *doer* or *agent of action*) does not need to be in the sentence. In contrast, for active voice, the *real subject* is also the *grammatical subject*. If that sounds complicated, a few examples will clear things up. Let's start by reviewing grammatical subjects and real subjects.

## Grammatical Subjects and Real Subjects

1. The grammatical subject precedes the verb.
2. The real subject drives the action of the verb.

In active voice, the grammatical subject and the real subject are the same, as shown below in italics.

**Active Voice:**   Jane's *manager* gave her a laptop.

In comparison, in the following passive sentence, the grammatical subject is *Jane*, and the real subject *manager* is in the object position:

**Passive Voice:**   *Jane* was given a laptop by her *manager*.

Since the real subject *manager* appears in the sentence, the above example is a *full passive*. In comparison, the following sentence has a grammatical subject, but not a real subject (a doer or agent of action):

**Passive Voice:**   A *laptop* was given to Jane.

In the example above, who gave Jane the laptop? When a passive sentence does not contain a real subject, it is called a *truncated passive*.

Now let's go over active voice from the beginning.

## Active Voice

Active voice is easier to understand through an example than an explanation, so let's revise a passive sentence to active voice.

**Passive:**      The papers were sent to Sue by Bob.

In the sentence above, the main verb is *sent*, and the real subject is *Bob*. Change the order in the sentence so that *Bob* becomes the grammatical subject, thereby driving the action of the verb.

**Active:**      Bob sent the papers to Sue.

Here are steps to revise a passive sentence to active voice:

**Step 1:**      Identify the **main verb** of the sentence.

**Step 2:**      Identify the **real subject** by asking,
              *who performed the action?*

**Step 3:**      Place the real subject (along with modifying words) at the beginning of the sentence (which is the position of the grammatical subject).

**Step 4:**      Follow the real subject with the verb, adjusting for agreement and tense.

**Step 5:**      Complete the sentence.

Let's revise another passive sentence to active voice.

**Passive:**      The merger was rejected by their new CEO.

**Step 1:**      What is the main verb?    *rejected*

**Step 2:**      Who performed the action:
              Who did the rejecting?    *Their new CEO*

**Steps 3 and 4:**    What is the real subject and verb?

*Their new CEO rejected . . .*

Along with the real subject and the verb, include any words that modify the real subject and adjust the verb for agreement and tense, if needed.

**Step 5:**    What is the complete sentence?

*Their new CEO rejected the merger.*

Using "shorthand," here is the process:

**Step 1:**    Main verb?
**Step 2:**    Real subject?
**Steps 3 and 4:**    Real subject + verb (*agreement and tense?*)
**Step 5:**    S – V – O.

**Here is the structure for the *active voice*:**

Who *did, does, or will do* what.

**Here is the structure for the *passive voice*:**

What *was done, is being done,* or *will be done* by whom.

This step-by-step analysis makes revising passive sentences to active voice sound simple. In fact, the process is simple, even with complex sentences. However, revising your thinking may be more difficult than revising your writing.

At first, you may have difficulty identifying your own passive sentences. That is partly because writing in a complicated way feels comfortable. Reading your own writing also feels comfortable because you are already familiar with your ideas. Instead, notice your reaction *as a reader* to various types of writing that others produce. As you build your awareness, analyze your own writing with an open mind, identifying your beliefs and fears about writing.

As you revise your writing, you may try to convince yourself that passive voice is more effective, partly because you think that it makes you sound smarter. The truth is, readers don't care about how smart you are; they are concerned about understanding the point that you are making in the moment.

When readers have difficulty understanding a message, they tend to dismiss it, if they can; if they can't, they struggle with it until they complete their task. At any rate, most people could not care less about how smart someone else is: they are far too busy worrying about how they present themselves and how others perceive them.

The best way to win friends and influence people is to make others feel smart. And let's face it, the best way to win friends and prove how smart you are is to make complicated ideas sound simple.

In conjunction with passive voice, writers often use nominalized verbs, another element that complicates writing unnecessarily.

## Nominalization

Would it surprise you to learn that most verbs have the potential to become nouns?

The word *nominal* refers to words that function as nouns. The term for transforming a verb into a noun is *nominalization*.[1] Many verbs turn into nominals by adding a suffix such as *−ment* or *−tion*. Here are some examples:

| Verbs | Nominals |
|---|---|
| accomplish | accomplishment |
| connect | connection |
| decide | decision |

| | |
|---|---|
| dedicate | dedication |
| develop | development |
| encourage | encouragement |
| evaluate | evaluation |
| verify | verification |

As some verbs become nominalized, they follow no specific pattern. For example, the verb *analyze* turns into the noun *analysis* . . . the verb *fail* turns into the noun *failure* . . . and the verb *maintain* turns into the noun *maintenance*.

Obviously, nouns have no action and, in general, words that originate as nouns cannot become verbs. When people use a noun as a verb, the construction often sounds awkward, as in "Let's *lunch* together" or "Do you *lotto*?" One word, however, plays a unique role in English grammar, and that word is *Google*. Google is a proper noun that also functions as a proper verb. Can you think of another proper noun that can also function as a verb?

By taking action out of the verb, nominalization changes a verb's DNA, so to speak, adding another layer of complication. However, nominalization can also add value when used effectively, just as passive voice adds value when used with purpose. And, let's be honest, isn't *nominalization* a word that you would rather avoid?

Here is an example of the verb *appreciate* and its nominalized form *appreciation*.

**Nominalized:**      I want to express my *appreciation* for your help.

**Active:**      I *appreciate* your help.

In the nominalized version above, the weak verb *want* replaces the strong verb *appreciate*. As well as stripping *appreciate* of its action, the nominalized version is more wordy. Here is another example using the verb *commit* and its nominalized form *commitment*:

**Nominalized/Passive:**

A *commitment* of resources for the *reconstruction* of our facility in New Orleans was made by our CEO.

**Active:**

Our CEO *committed* resources for *reconstructing* our facility in New Orleans.

For the most part, as writing becomes more complicated, it also becomes less effective. When you edit, remain aware of nominals, and make sure that you are using them purposefully, just as you would use the passive voice with purpose.

When writers cling to the passive voice and nominalizations, they may mistakenly believe that they sound sophisticated. However, unnecessarily long four-syllable words do not improve the flow of writing. Judge for yourself; here is one more example:

**Nominalized/Passive:**

*Encouragement* was given to me by my coach and teammates.

**Passive:**

I *was encouraged* by my coach and teammates.

**Active:**

My coach and teammates *encouraged* me.

The first sentence is passive and uses the nominalized form of the verb *encourage,* which is *encouragement.* In the second sentence, the nominal becomes a verb, but the sentence is still passive. In the third sentence, *encourage* is an active verb in its past tense form.

At times, nominalizations work well, for example:

> I value your *appreciation.*

By removing the nominalization, you would need to express the same sentiment as follows, which sounds awkward:

> When you appreciate my work, I value it.

Make complex messages as simple as you can: use nominalizations only when they improve the quality of your writing, and use passive voice only when it improves the tone of your writing.

Understanding these principles intellectually is much easier than applying them to your own writing. To keep your writing active, remain open minded and diligent. The more committed you are, the more effective your writing will become.

## Style, Tone, and Meaning

One of the biggest arguments against letting go of the passive voice is that revising a passive sentence to active voice changes its meaning.

Shifting from one voice to another does not change the meaning, but it can change the tone. When all actors are present in a sentence, changing from passive to active voice is an exercise in translation.

The passive voice is indirect and somewhat abstract because the person or thing performing the described action does not even need to be present.

For example, how many times have you heard sentences such as the following:

**Passive**: The problem will be solved.

A solution will be developed.

Who is solving the problem? Who is developing a solution?

The passive voice allows people to say things without ascribing responsibility for actions. In addition, with passive voice, writers do not connect with their own words in the way that they must with active voice, for example:

**Passive**: A discussion of the issue ensued at length before an acceptable compromise could be established.

Once again, who discussed the issue? By adding people to the mix, the sentence becomes much more reader-friendly.

**Active**: We discussed the issue at length before we reached a compromise.

Though passive voice sounds more formal than active voice, today's culture no longer supports that kind of artificial, distant formality.

Any kind of change is difficult, and that includes changing your style of writing. Breaking out of an academic or a corporate mold takes courage, commitment, and vigilance.

In fact, if you start writing in the active voice, your associates are not likely to notice the change unless it is to appreciate your clear, direct writing style. But there is one important reason to use the passive voice, and that's when tact is called for.

## Passive Voice, the Tactful Voice

The passive voice is perfect for situations that have the potential to involve blame, for example:

**Passive:**    A mistake was made on the August invoice.

George was not informed that the incident was reported.

The check was not deposited in time to avert an overdraft.

The client was not consulted about the account change.

Passive voice allows you to focus on the problem and not the person. If you use the passive voice when giving constructive feedback, the listener is more likely to take the message objectively.

## Recap

Revising passive sentences to active voice improves the quality and readability of writing, but does not necessarily change the meaning.

Stay vigilant in your quest to write actively: active voice brings writing to life so that it produces results.

## Action Steps

What are your *takeaways*? What key points do you plan to apply?

-------------------------------------------------------------------

-------------------------------------------------------------------

-------------------------------------------------------------------

### Reference

1.    Joseph M. Williams, *Style: Toward Clarity and Grace*, The University of Chicago Press, 1990.

# 7

# Know Your Viewpoint

No one writes perfectly, and no one speaks perfectly—it's not even possible, and that is partly due to pronouns. Pronouns are a core element of writing, and most writers struggle with them. At times, writers make their writing more complicated just to avoid pronouns.

When you compose, it is natural to speak from the *I* viewpoint. When you edit, shift to the *you* viewpoint. By speaking directly to your reader, you bring your writing to life.

In addition to using the *I* viewpoint unnecessarily, writers make the common error of using pronouns inconsistently, going back and forth between different voices; for example:

*I* like to jog because it's good for *you*.

Because pronouns must agree with their antecedents, at times writers construct award-sounding sentences to be correct, such as:

*A professional* should always do *his or her* best.

When you find your comfort zone with pronouns, you will be that much closer to finding your own voice.

Let's first examine how to produce reader-friendly writing by using the *you* viewpoint then review how to use pronouns correctly and consistently.

## The *You* Viewpoint

When you compose, your words need to flow freely; so even if you start every sentence with *I*, that's acceptable. Compose for yourself, then edit for your reader.

When you edit, shift your thinking to your reader by shifting from the *I* viewpoint to the *you* viewpoint.

*I* **Viewpoint:**   *I* am writing to let you know that *I* would like to invite you to our next meeting.

*You* **Viewpoint:**   Would *you* be interested in attending our next meeting?

By speaking directly to your reader through the *you* viewpoint, you engage your reader and tune in to your reader's needs. Here are more examples:

*I* **Viewpoint:**   *I* am writing to ask you about the new policy.
*I* would like to know what you think about the change.
*I* would like to encourage you to apply for the new position.

*You* **Viewpoint:**   *(You)* Please tell me about the new policy.
What do *you* think about the change?
*You* should apply for the new position.

At times, the subject of a sentence is implied or understood, as in the first *you* viewpoint example above. The *you understood* subject is represented as *(you)*.

In fact, English has two types of implied subjects: *you understood* and *I understood*. Here are examples:

### *You Understood* Subject:

> (You) Stop at the front desk before you leave.
>
> (You) Take a seat in the front row, if you wish.

### *I Understood* Subject:

> (I) Thank you.
>
> (I) Hope you are having a great day.

"Thank you" is a complete sentence because it has a subject and a verb and expresses a complete thought. The next time that you close an e-mail saying *thank you*, follow it with a period rather than a comma: "Thank you."

As an aside, the word *thanks* can also be considered a complete sentence. That is because in English words that play a structural role remain part of the sentence structure even when removed, becoming understood or implied. When you say "thanks," you are actually saying an abbreviated version of "I give thanks to you."

By putting the focus on your reader, the *you* viewpoint also improves the tone of your document. Here are a few more examples:

**I Viewpoint:**    *I* am writing you to ask about my account.

*I* appreciate the job you did on the proposal.

*I* appreciated your help with the Baker job.

**You Viewpoint:**    Could *you* answer a few questions about my account?

*You* did a great job on the proposal.

*You* helped me when you assisted with the Baker job.

As stated, the *you* viewpoint helps readers stay connected because they feel as if the writer is speaking directly to them. However, the *I* viewpoint is effective and even necessary at times, so do not try to eliminate every sentence that begins with *I*.

In fact, you will find yourself overusing the passive voice if you avoid using *I* completely. Therefore, when you write from your own experience, use the *I* point of view.

**I Viewpoint**:       *I* completed the project last week.

By avoiding the *I* viewpoint, you would need to write passively:

**Passive**:       The project was completed last week.

                The completion of the project occurred last week.

Since the *I* viewpoint engages the reader more effectively, choose the *I* viewpoint over the passive voice, unless you are trying to be tactful.

An extension of the *I* viewpoint is the *editorial we*. The *we* viewpoint is effective because it allows business writers to stress that they represent their company, as in the following:

**We Viewpoint**:    *We* appreciate your business—please let *us* know if there is anything *we* can do to make your stay more comfortable.

Now let us look at how to make writing flow well by using pronouns correctly and consistently.

# Pronoun and Antecedent Agreement

A pronoun is used in place of a noun or another pronoun, and the word or words that it refers to are known as **antecedents**.

In the following example, *managers* is the antecedent of *they* and *their*:

> All *managers* said that *they* would submit *their* quarterly reports before the 30th of the month.

Pronouns must agree with their antecedents in number and gender. Many antecedents are gender neutral, such as person, doctor, engineer, lawyer, teacher, and so on, which creates a unique problem for writers.

When writers use singular antecedents that are gender neutral, such as "a person," English does not provide choices that allow writing to flow naturally. Instead, writers must use combinations of pronouns, such as *he or she* and *him or her*. In the following example, the antecedent *broker* is gender neutral:

**Correct:** When a *broker* performs *his* or *her* duties, *he* or *she* must remain attentive to *his* or *her* clients.

When using singular antecedents, writers are prone to make errors with pronouns. For example, many writers would have erred on the above sentence by using plural pronouns, such as *they* and *their*.

**Incorrect:** When *a broker* performs *their* duties, *they* must remain attentive to *their* clients.

To avoid the awkwardness of using *he or she* and *his or her* with singular antecedents (and simultaneously avoid the type of error shown above), use plural antecedents.

**Corrected:**    When *brokers* perform *their* duties *they* must remain attentive to *their* clients.

Here are a few more examples:

**Incorrect:**    When a *pilot* flies, *they* need to stay focused.
**Corrected:**
   **Singular**    When a *pilot* flies, *he* or *she* needs to stay focused.
   **Plural**    When *pilots* fly, *they* need to stay focused.

**Incorrect:**    Every *team member* should bring *their* own *laptop*.
**Corrected:**
   **Singular**    Every *team member* should bring *his* or *her* own *laptop*.
   **Plural**    All *team members* should bring *their* own *laptops*.

Notice in the above example that *laptops* becomes plural right along with *team members*. Consistency and agreement apply to all related elements. Here's another example of agreement in number:

**Incorrect:**    The *children* brought their *lunch* to school.
**Corrected:**    The *children* brought their *lunches* to school.

Another issue arises in sentences that contain more than one antecedent. When two or more antecedents appear in a sentence, pronoun reference can be unclear.

For example, in the following sentence, which person does the pronoun *she* refer to?

**Unclear:**           *Sue and Martha* completed *their* report by Tuesday so that *she* could present the findings at a conference on Thursday.

When meaning is unclear, restate the antecedent instead of using a pronoun.

**Clear:**           *Sue and Martha* completed *their* report by Tuesday so that *Martha* could present the findings at a conference on Thursday.

Here is a slightly more complicated example:

**Unclear:**           *Charley* said that *John* should be on his team because *he* would be available to help *him* during *his* training.

**Clear:**           *Charley* said that *John* should be on his team because *Charley* would be available to help *John* during *his* (or *John's* ) training.

## Point of View and Consistency

As part of your editing process, screen your writing to ensure that you are writing from a specific point of view; stay consistent with that point of view within sentences, paragraphs, and even entire documents.

Point of view, or pronoun viewpoint, emanates from first, second, or third person, singular or plural.

Here are examples of the various viewpoints:

When *I* speak, *I* must pay attention to *my* audience.
When *you* speak, *you* must pay attention to *your* audience.
When a *person* speaks, *he* or *she* must pay attention to *his* or *her* audience.
When *we* speak, *we* must pay attention to *our* audience.
When *people* speak, *they* must pay attention to *their* audience.

Though the *one* viewpoint is not common in the United States, other English-speaking countries commonly use the *one* viewpoint.

**For example:**    When *one* speaks, *one* must pay attention to *one's* audience.

An error many writers make, however, is to mix the pronoun *one* with other viewpoints, especially when they are unsure of pronoun choice, as shown in the next example.

**Incorrect:**    *I* think *one* should write daily so that *you* improve *your* skills.

Do not shift point of view within sentences or paragraphs. Here are various ways that you could correct the above sentence:

**Corrected:**    *I* should write daily so that *I* improve *my* skills.
*You* should write daily so that *you* improve your skills.
*One* should write daily so that *one* improves *one's* skills.

Here are more examples of shifting viewpoint:

**Incorrect:** If *a person* arrives on time, *they* will receive good service.

**Corrected:** If *a person* arrives on time, *he* or *she* will receive good service.

If people arrive on time, *they* will receive good service.

If *you* arrive on time, *you* will receive good service.

**Incorrect:** *An employee* should follow the policy so that *you* treat *your* clients fairly.

**Corrected:** *An employee* should follow the policy so that *he* or *she* treats *his* or *her* clients fairly.

Even though the above sentence is correct, notice how tedious it is to present it in third person singular. A better choice would be making the antecedent plural or using the *you* viewpoint, as shown in the examples that follow.

**Corrected:** *Employees* should follow the policy so that *they* treat *their* clients fairly.

*(You)* Follow the policy so that *you* treat *your* clients fairly.

The point of view you select helps you adapt your topic to your audience. The *you* viewpoint is especially important for business writing because it allows you to speak directly to your client. In fact, at times, readers do not take action or answer questions because a statement sounds indirect or vague, for example:

| Weak: | Applications must be completed and submitted by the June deadline so that enrollment can occur in the current calendar year. |
|---|---|
| Revised: | (You) Please submit your application by June 5 so that you can enroll this year. |
| Weak: | I need to know the information about seminar attendance before the deadline. |
| Revised: | (You) Please let me know by May 7 who will be attending the seminar. |

Once you select a point of view, use that point of view consistently.

## A Few Tips about *Subjects* and *Objects*

One of the biggest mistakes that people make with pronouns is using a formal-sounding pronoun such as *I* in place of a less formal-sounding pronoun such as *me*. That kind of mistake is known as a *hypercorrection*.

Hypercorrection is common. Unsure speakers pick up incorrect pronoun use almost the way they would pick up a virus, changing their speech so that it sounds right. If you want to use pronouns correctly, base your decisions on how they *function* in a sentence and not how others use them; then you will have sound and principle on your side.

Your first step in gaining control of pronouns lies in using subjective case and objective case pronouns correctly. At the core of pronoun use, here is the question you need to answer:

Does the pronoun function as a *subject* or as an *object*?

## PRONOUN CASE

| | Subjective | Objective | Possessive | Reflexive |
|---|---|---|---|---|
| **Singular** | | | | |
| 1$^{st}$ Person | I | me | my, mine | myself |
| 2$^{nd}$ Person | you | you | your, yours | yourself |
| 3$^{rd}$ Person | he | him | his | himself |
| | she | her | hers | herself |
| | it | it | its | itself |
| **Plural** | | | | |
| 1$^{st}$ Person | we | us | our, ours | ourselves |
| 2$^{nd}$ Person | you | you | your, yours | yourselves |
| 3$^{rd}$ Person | they | them | their, theirs | themselves |

Here is a summary of the role that each case plays in a sentence:

- *Subjective* case pronouns function as *subjects* of verbs, and thus a subjective case pronoun is used as the subject of a sentence.

- *Objective* case pronouns function as *objects*, usually of verbs or prepositions.

- *Possessive* case pronouns *show possession* of nouns or other pronouns.

- *Reflexive* case pronouns reflect back to subjective case pronouns; reflexive case pronouns are also known as *intensive case pronouns*.

Here is why many writers make mistakes with subjective case and objective case pronouns:

1.  Subjective case pronouns sound more formal than objective case pronouns. An unsure speaker will use *I* or *he* as an object, when *me* or *him* would be correct.

2.  When a pronoun is part of a pair, incorrect pronoun use can sound correct.

Here are some examples:

**Incorrect:**  Bill asked Mike and *I* to assist him.

**Correct:**  Bill asked Mike and *me* to assist him.

**Incorrect:**  George and *me* went to the game last Friday.

**Correct:**  George and *I* went to the game last Friday.

In place of a subjective case pronoun or an objective case pronoun, some writers incorrectly substitute a reflexive case pronoun.

**Incorrect:**  George and *myself* went to the game last Friday.

**Incorrect:**  Bill asked Mike and *myself* to assist him.

**Incorrect:**  Sue and *yourself* can work on the project.

Instead, use a reflexive case pronoun only when it refers to a subjective case pronoun or a noun already in the sentence.

Here are some examples using reflexive case pronouns correctly:

*I* will do the work *myself*.

*You* can complete the project *yourself*, if you have the time.

*Susan* referred to *herself* as the person in charge of hiring.

The *dog* bit *itself* in the foot, mistaking his foot for a bone!

To use subjective case and objective case pronouns correctly, first identify whether the pronoun functions as a *subject* or as an *object*. If the pronoun stands alone, it is easier to test by sound.

If the pronoun is part of a pair, use the following substitutions:

1. Use *I* if you could substitute *we*:

   *Sam and I* went to the game: *We* went to the game.

2. Use *me* if you could substitute *us*:

   Sally asked *Juan and me* for help: Sally asked *us* for help.

3. Use *he* or *she* if you could substitute *they*:

   *Martin and he* finished the project: *they* finished the project.

4. Use *him* or *her* if you could substitute *them*:

   Melissa encouraged *Jamie and her* to go: Melissa encouraged *them*.

Another way would be to simplify your sentence by taking out the other person and then testing for sound.

Using the previous examples above, here is how you would test your pronoun based on sound:

**Incorrect:**   Sam and *me* went to the game.

**Simplify:**   ~~Sam and~~ *me* went to the game.

**Correct:**   Sam and *I* went to the game.


**Incorrect:**   Sally asked Juan and *I* for help.

**Simplify:**   Sally asked ~~Juan and~~ *I* for help.

**Correct:**   Sally asked Juan and *me* for help.


**Incorrect:**   Martin and *him* finished the project.

**Simplify:**   ~~Martin and~~ *him* finished the project.

**Correct:**   Martin and *he* finished the project.


**Incorrect:**   Bill asked Mike and *myself* to assist him.

**Simplify:**   Bill asked ~~Mike and~~ *myself* to assist him.

**Correct:**   Bill asked Mike and *me* to assist him.


Using pronouns correctly improves writing as well as speech.

## Business Writing Versus Academic Writing

The discipline in which you are writing dictates pronoun usage, and business writing differs from academic and scientific writing in important ways.

While most business writing occurs in context with the goal of connecting directly with the reader, much of academic and scientific writing involves summarizing results.

When summarizing an article, you would not speak from your own point of view; instead, you would speak from the author's point of view. Let us say you are summarizing an article on economic theory by George Jones. You would write from the third person singular point of view when you discuss what Jones discovered and when you discuss economic theory; for example:

> *Jones* reports that the data indicates a rise in consumer spending.
> *He* further concludes that . . .
> *Jones* argues that the economy . . .
> The *economy* can be . . .

Notice that you are not speaking directly to the reader nor are you giving your personal feelings or beliefs about the topic. By discussing points that you think that the reader will find of interest, you are connecting to the reader in an indirect way, not in a direct way.

When speaking from a personal viewpoint is not a viable option, writers rely on the passive voice; passive voice is an accepted element of academic and scientific writing. Therefore, when you write in one of these more formal genres, pay attention to viewpoint, generally avoiding the *I* or *you* viewpoint.

To learn more about academic writing, see the college edition of this book, *Writing in College: Faster, Better, and Smarter.*

## Recap

Once again, screen for correct pronoun use while you edit, not while you compose. If you worry about pronoun usage as you compose, you are likely to walk away from your project!

By using pronouns correctly and consistently, you are ensuring that your documents are professional and reader-friendly. The following points relate to business writing:

1. The *you* viewpoint is preferred to the *I* viewpoint.
2. The *I* viewpoint is generally preferred to the passive voice.
3. Business writers use the *editorial we* to convey that they are acting as a representative of their company.
4. Pronouns must agree in number and gender with their antecedents.
5. One key to using pronouns consistently with their antecedents is to use plural antecedents.

To make sure that you are using subjective and objective case pronouns correctly—ask, is it a *subject* or an *object*?

## Action Steps

What are your *takeaways*? What key points do you plan to apply?

# 8

# Be Concise

As a wise writer once said, "This would be shorter if I had more time." No doubt, the additional time would be spent editing.

A first step in editing is cutting excess, which begins after you have clear insight into your purpose. Your insight and clarity are cues that you are ready to shift from composing to editing.

Even seasoned writers struggle with their words until their thoughts become clear, and those moments are magical: the insights, the clarity, the next step revealed. Adapt your expectations so that they are in line with the reality of the writing process, and writing will not disappoint you. Writing develops your thinking: compose fearlessly until you understand your point. Then edit your writing so that you say what you mean in the simplest, most concise way.

To get rid of clutter, you may need to change some ways of thinking and give up canned phrases that give you comfort, such as *per your request* or *thank you in advance*. Also consider:

1. Simple words and short messages convey information more effectively than complex words and long messages.

2. Using big, four-syllable words is not a sign of intelligence.

As you let go of artificial, abstract, and outdated language, you are closer to finding your voice and bringing your writing to life for your reader. So let's get started.

# Eliminate Redundant Pairings

Redundant modifiers result from the unconscious use of outdated language that crept into English centuries ago, for example:

- The ~~true and accurate~~ facts . . .
- First ~~and foremost,~~ . . .

If a fact is not "true and accurate," it isn't a fact. And if you list something first, isn't it also foremost? Another example is "various and sundry": do you even know what *sundry* means?

Though redundant pairings seem to fit together like bookends, you need only one of the words; and when you use both, you are automatically and unconsciously . . . *oops, is that a redundant pairing?*

For the following pairings, which word would you cut? If you can, cover the revised words as you go through the original list.

| Original | Revised |
|---|---|
| and so on and so forth | and so on |
| any and all | any *or* all |
| basic and fundamental | basic |
| each and every | each *or* every |
| fair and equitable | fair |
| first and foremost | first |
| full and complete | complete |
| if and when | if *or* when |
| hopes and desires | hopes |
| hope and trust | trust |
| issues and concerns | issues |
| more and more | more |
| null and void | void |

| | |
|---|---|
| questions and problems | questions |
| true and accurate | accurate |
| this day and age | today |
| thoughts and ideas | thoughts *or* ideas |

Also cut unnecessary verb add ons:

| Verb Add Ons | Revised |
|---|---|
| add up | add |
| add together | add |
| advance forward | advance |
| continue on | continue |
| combine together | combine |
| refer back | refer |
| repeat again | repeat |
| rise up | rise |

Another type of redundancy that seems to be built into the language is redundant modifiers.

## Cut Redundant Modifiers

Some words simply do not need to be modified. For example, have you ever wondered about *free gifts*? If gifts are not free, are they still gifts? What about *sudden crisis* and *advance reservations*? Aren't all crises sudden and all reservations made in advance?

Redundant modifiers come in all shapes and sizes, so you may chuckle as you go through the following exercise. Cover the revised list as you cut the redundant modifiers in the original list.

| Original | Revised |
|---|---|
| advance warning | warning |
| close proximity | close |
| cold temperature | cold |
| combine together | combine |
| completely demolished | demolished |
| completely eliminate | eliminate |
| completely finish | finish |
| difficult dilemma | dilemma |
| each individual | each |
| end result | result |
| exactly identical | identical |
| final outcome | outcome |
| foreign imports | imports |
| frozen ice | frozen, ice |
| future plans | plans |
| general public | public |
| honest truth | truth |
| most perfect | perfect |
| new breakthrough | breakthrough |
| one hundred percent true | true |
| personal beliefs | beliefs |
| sudden crisis | crisis |
| true facts | facts |
| tuna fish | tuna |
| unexpected surprise | surprise |
| very unique | unique |
| 12 noon/12 midnight | noon *or* midnight |

Have you identified any redundant modifiers that you use on a regular basis?

## Cut Vague Nouns

Do you use vague nouns? For example, nouns such as *area, factor, manner, situation, topic,* and even *purpose* are easy to use as fillers during the composing phase. Say what you mean and be specific.

**Wordy:**    My purpose for writing is to give you information about our new program.

**Revised:**   Our new program offers you many options . . .

**Wordy:**    I have found myself in a situation in which I am forced to make a decision.

**Revised:**   I am forced to make a decision.

**Wordy:**    The topic that we discussed at your last meeting was revised HR policies.

**Revised:**   At our last meeting, we discussed revised HR policies.

Can you think of any vague nouns that you use?

## Eliminate the Obvious

Isn't *round* a shape and *red* a color? As a 14<sup>th</sup> century Franciscan monk named William of Ockham is credited for saying, "Plurality should not be posited without necessity."

Go through the list below, cutting the obvious, as modeled by the first few below.

round ~~in shape~~              consensus of opinion

audible ~~to the ear~~         brief in duration

| period of time | soft to the touch |
| visible to the eye | filled to capacity |
| bright in color | re-elected for another term |
| red in color | honest in character |

In fact, when you find yourself using the following phrases, simply delete them and get right to your point:

all things considered
as a matter of fact
as far as I am concerned
for the most part
for the purpose of
for all intents and purposes
I wish to take this opportunity
in a manner of speaking
in my opinion
my purpose for writing is
the point I am trying to make
what I am trying to say is that
what I want to make clear is

Next, let's look at getting rid of canned and outdated phrases.

## Update Outdated Phrases

Outdated phrases are like viruses, and writers pick them up easily from colleagues they respect. For example, phrases such as *thank you in advance* (which can sound presumptuous) and *per your suggestion* have been outdated for more than 30 years now. Even so, writers still use these outdated phrases daily.

Remember:

*If you wouldn't say it that way, don't write it that way.*

Be confident about your writing and stop using outdated phrases, even if someone you respect still uses them. Once again, cover the right column that shows current use as you work through the outdated column. (And yes, it is somewhat painful to give up a word such as *per* if you've been using it every day for years.)

| **Outdated** | **Current** |
|---|---|
| as per our discussion | as we discussed |
| as per your request | as you requested |
| at all times | always |
| at the present time | now, today |
| at your earliest convenience | *give a specific date* |
| attached please find | attached is |
| due to the fact that | because |
| during the time that | while |
| gave a report to the effect | reported |
| gave assistance to | helped |
| in the event that | if |
| in a situation in which | when |
| in almost every instance | usually |
| in the near future | soon |
| in receipt of | Thank you for . . . |
| in reference to | about |
| is of the opinion that | believes |
| I wish to thank you | *don't wish, just thank* |
| may I suggest | *don't ask permission to suggest* |
| prior to | before |

| | |
|---|---|
| subsequent to | after |
| sufficient number of | enough |
| thank you in advance | thank you |
| thank you again | *one thank you is sufficient* |
| the manner in which | how |
| this day and age | today |
| with regard to | about *or* concerning |

In addition to being outdated, *thank you in advance* can sound presumptuous. Also, do not use *thank you* as an automatic closing in an e-mail: say *thank you* in response to someone assisting you.

## Avoid Legalese

At one time, attorneys filled their writing with legalese. However, today even many attorneys avoid using the following terms.

| Legalese | Revised |
|---|---|
| as stated heretofore | as stated |
| aforementioned | as mentioned |
| concerning the matter of | concerning |
| enclosed herewith please find | enclosed is |
| enclosed herein | enclosed is |
| notwithstanding | without |
| pursuant to | regarding |
| the writer/the undersigned | use *I* or *me* |
| until such time as | until |

Words are choices. When you find yourself using outdated language, read your writing out loud—hearing the way words ring in your ears is a motivating way to revise your writing.

## Modify Sparingly

With creative writing, detail supports the reader's experience; with business writing, unnecessary detail creates frustration. Two kinds of modifiers that creep into writing are **hedges** and **emphatics**.

- *Hedges* are words that writers use to qualify a statement; use them only when they are necessary, for example:

  This principle is ~~kind of~~ important if you are writing a book.

- *Emphatics* are words that writers use to stress a point, but the emphatic has the opposite effect, for example:

  The meeting is ~~very~~ important, and you ~~really~~ need to be there.

**Here are some common hedges to avoid**:

kind of, sort of, rarely, hardly, at times, tend, sometimes, maybe, may be, perhaps, in my opinion, more or less, possibly, probably, seemingly,  to a certain extent, supposedly, usually, often, almost always

**Here are some common emphatics; use them sparingly**:

very, most, many, often, really, literally, virtually, usually, certainly, inevitably, as you can plainly see, as everyone is aware, as you know, always, each and every time, totally, it is quite clear that, as you may already know, absolutely, undoubtedly, first and foremost

**Example with hedges and emphatics:**

*For the most part*, trust is best established from the beginning and *really* difficult to regain once breached. *First and foremost*, assume that *each and every* communication *may* have the potential to build trust as well as the potential to destroy trust.

**Example without hedges or emphatics:**

Trust is best established from the beginning and difficult to regain once breached. Always assume that every communication has the potential to build trust as well as the potential to destroy trust.

## Avoid Fillers

The words *just* and *like* are not modifiers--they are known as fillers. These words creep into casual speech and writing.

| | |
|---|---|
| **Incorrect:** | He *like* gave me a great recommendation. |
| **Corrected:** | He gave me a great recommendation. |
| | |
| **Incorrect:** | She *like just* told me the correct information yesterday. |
| **Corrected:** | She told me the correct information yesterday. |

In fact, job interviewers discount applicants who use fillers such as *like* and *just* in their speech. Cutting a few select words makes a difference.

## Modify Correctly

Modifying phrases take as their subject the noun closest to them. When you use modifying phrases, place the modifying phrase close to the noun it modifies.

**Misplaced modifier**:  Bert is the *person* across the room *with the navy pinstriped suit*.

**Corrected**:  Bert is the *person in the navy pinstriped suit* across the room.

What does the following sentence actually say?

**Dangling modifier**:  While answering the phone, *Jill's coffee* spilled.

In other words, was *Jill's coffee* answering the phone?

**Corrected**:  As Jill answered the phone, she spilled her coffee.
While answering the phone, Jill spilled her coffee.

Many dangling modifiers go unnoticed, and some can be quite amusing.

## Edit Out Background Thinking

As you compose, you may go through a lot of detail to get to your main point. That kind of background thinking serves a purpose while you are composing, but cut it when you edit.

Get practice by editing the examples on the next page, cutting background thinking.

**Example 1:**

After we spoke, I continued to think about the situation in which we find ourselves. Not that long ago, the economy was strong, and we were looking for different ways to invest our profits. Now, with the sudden change in the economy, we are faced with uncertainty—many of our clients will be tightening their belts and reducing their spending. With a possible impending budget shortfall, don't you think we should revise the budget now instead of waiting until next quarter? What do you think?

*What is the key point of the above message? How much can you cut?*

........................................................................

........................................................................

........................................................................

**Example 2:**

I'm not sure if you are going to like this idea, but I've been thinking about this for a few weeks now, tossing over the pros and cons. Generally our productivity goes down by the last day of our sales meeting—everyone is tired and distracted and ready to go home. They are also over-saturated with great ideas and need time to process them. I think we could cut the sales meeting by one day this summer. By doing so, I believe that we could save about 20 percent of our costs and probably accomplish just as much in the shorter time frame. Let me know what you think.

*What is the key point in Example 2? Which sentences can you cut?*

........................................................................

........................................................................

........................................................................

(See page 112 for suggested answers.)

When you edit, cut beliefs and opinions, as appropriate; also, when you can, leave out phrases such as *I believe*, *I think*, and *I feel;* you will sound more confident.

## Recap

Do not presume that big words or lengthy phrases impress readers. Keep your writing simple and to the point.

1. Put purpose first, and you will have a clear idea of what to cut.
2. Use updated words and phrases, and revise complicated phrases to more simple terms.
3. Modify sparingly, cutting hedges and emphatics.
4. Edit out your background thinking and opinions.
5. Be direct and say what you mean.

Give yourself freedom to compose—cut when you edit and revise.

## Action Steps

What are your *takeaways*? What key points do you plan to apply?

*Key to Example 1, page 110:* Considering the poor economy and that we might have a budget shortfall, should we revise the budget now instead of waiting until next quarter? What do you think?

*Key to Example 2, page 110:* Generally our productivity goes down by the last day of the summer sales meeting. If we cut the sales meeting by one day this summer, we could save about 20 percent and probably accomplish just as much in less time. What do you think?

# 9

# Fine-Tune Your Tone

Tone is not as much about *what you say* as about *how you say it*. Simple, accessible messages set an effective tone, whereas long, complicated messages do not.

In addition, just as there are at least two sides to every story, there are two sides to tone:

> *Tone is not just about how a writer conveys a message—*
> *it's also about how the reader interprets it.*

Though you do not have control over how others interpret your message, you do have control over how you interpret theirs. Have you ever read a message that sounded accusatory or negative? Did your reaction change after you read the message again later?

Whether you are sending or receiving a message, notice how your feelings play into the dynamic. For example, when you are having a bad day, do you tend to be more abrupt and feel more sensitive toward how others convey their messages?

Reading too much into the written word can create problems: if you infer that there is a problem, you may actually create one. By giving others *the benefit of the doubt*, you also save yourself from unnecessary frustration.

Tone can either enhance a relationship or tear it down. Let's look at a few ways to set an effective tone.

# Be Positive

Everyone appreciates positive words; even subtle comments add energy. To stay positive, focus on *what will go right if procedures are followed* rather than on what will go wrong if they are not.

In fact, even valuable services can sound threatening if stated in the negative, for example:

**Negative:**    If I don't hear from you within a week, I'll assume you are not interested.

**Positive:**    If you are interested, please contact me within the next week.

Another way to improve tone is to avoid the word *not*:

**Negative:**    You cannot schedule any time off until you complete the project.

**Positive:**    Once you complete the project, you can take time off.

Whenever you edit a sentence so that you state the same message without the word *not*, the tone sounds more positive.

**Negative:**    You are not qualified for the position.
**Positive:**    You are better qualified for other positions and would benefit from exploring other options.

When a situation is inviting, people are more inclined to put positive energy toward accomplishing the task.

# Use Clear, Accurate Language

Slang, jargon, and abbreviations affect tone on many levels, often having a negative effect.

E-mail is not the same communication tool as text messaging. When business professionals write e-mail messages as if they are text messages, they are sending their readers a multitude of unintended micro-messages. To respect your audience, also avoid colloquial phrases such as "bite the bullet" and "written in sand," which can be challenging for people from diverse cultures to understand.

Beyond avoiding jargon and clichés, also avoid telling jokes and using sarcasm. You have no idea how your reader will respond, and you have no idea to whom your reader may forward your message.

Even traditional abbreviations presented as *acronyms* or *initialisms* can be difficult for new employees to understand.

- An *acronym* is an abbreviation that can be spoken as a word, such as AARP or MADD.
- An *initialism* consists of the first letter of each word, such as NBC for National Broadcasting Company.

When you work with new employees, limit shortcuts. When using abbreviations, put the abbreviation in parentheses after the name:

> The Accounts Receivable Department (ARD) will
> answer your request. Although the ARD is closed for
> the holidays, you can reach them after January 2.

Or, you can use a less traditional format, putting the full name in parentheses following the abbreviation:

> The ARD (Accounts Receivable Department) will answer
> your request. . . .

The point is, the first time that you use any acronym or initialism in your writing, spell out the words in full. You will save your reader time and frustration. Everything that you do to make your message easier for your reader improves tone.

## Use Simple Language

Some people think that they sound smarter by using complicated words rather than simple ones. However, savvy writers choose simple words.

| Outdated | Revised |
|---|---|
| apprise | inform |
| ascertain | find out |
| cognizant of | aware of |
| contingent upon | dependent on |
| deem | think |
| endeavor | try |
| facilitate | help |
| implement | start, begin |
| initiate | begin |
| is desirous of | wants |
| methodology | method |
| prior to | before |
| render | make, give |
| render assistance | assist |
| referred to as | called |
| termination | end |
| transpire | happen |
| transmit | send |
| utilization | use |

**Instead of saying this:**

> We *utilize* that vendor.
>
> I am *cognizant of* the change.
>
> We *endeavor* to give the best service.
>
> *Prior to* working at Macy's . . .

**Say this:**

> We *use* that vendor.
>
> I am *aware* of the change.
>
> We *try* to give the best service.
>
> *Before* working at Macy's . . .

Though getting rid of outdated language is exhilarating, it is also as difficult as giving up a security blanket.

## Give Constructive Feedback

Honest feedback leading to growth can be difficult to hear, but feedback can also be difficult to give.

Below is a template to use to give constructive feedback:

**Positive – Constructive – Supportive (PCS) Feedback:**

1. Start with an honest, *positive* statement,
2. State the *constructive* feedback, and finally,
3. End on a *supportive* note.

By starting out with a positive comment, the recipient is more likely to listen and be receptive. Using questions also keeps the discussion open so that you can get at core issues.

Here's an example of PCS feedback:

> Peggy,
>
> In the past 6 months, you have done a great job bringing in new accounts.
>
> However, two of your long-standing clients have recently left to go with other ad agencies. One of them said it was due to your unavailability. Will you be able to adjust your schedule to meet the new demands of your increased client base?
>
> Do you need additional support?
>
> Don

By putting information in writing after your discussion, you have documentation; but more important, your summary helps ensure that you both have the same understanding; for example:

> Peggy,
>
> As a follow-up to our meeting about your schedule, please let me know if the following still works for you:
>
> - When you will be unavailable to receive calls for an entire day, you will let Roger or me know so that we can screen for important messages.
> - When you will be out of the office for more than a day, you will program your e-mail account with an out-of-office message, alerting clients that they can call Roger or me for immediate assistance.
>
> Please let me know how this works for you.
>
> Don

By following a pattern of comments that are *positive*, then *constructive*, and finally *supportive*, you are giving the other person the benefit of the doubt. Everyone appreciates support and deserves at least one second chance.

## Apologize Quickly

Finally, if you need to say *I'm sorry*, say it; but say it tactfully.

**Don't Say**: Please forgive me for making such a stupid error. You are such a valuable client, and I'm hoping we can mend the fences and get back on track.

**Don't Say**: Clearly you didn't understand what I was saying, or you wouldn't have reacted so strongly.

**Do Say**: Thank you for letting me know about this issue. I am sorry that this has caused you an inconvenience, and I have taken immediate steps to correct it.

Unless discussed directly, some issues will not go away. Addressing issues in a timely way can also keep additional challenges from taking root.

## Recap

Tone is a broad and varied topic. To develop an effective tone, apply the following in your writing:

1. Focus on the positive by stressing what will go right if procedures are followed rather than what will go wrong if they are not.

2.  When you give constructive feedback, follow the PCS format: start with a positive comment as it sets a supportive tone.

When a message strikes you the wrong way, clarify the message, as you may be misinterpreting the tone. Remember, if you infer there is a problem, you may actually create one.

## Action Steps

What are your *takeaways*? What key points do you plan to apply?

_____

_____

_____

_____

_____

# 10

# Be Sensitive to Diverse Styles

To understand others, you must first tune in to your own style and preferences. Otherwise, you may read too much into differences in communication styles, especially styles that are unlike your own. In fact, only by understanding your own style will you have insight into how to adapt to another's style.

For example, when you deal with people who have similar styles and backgrounds as your own, measure your decisions against the *Golden Rule*:

*Do unto others as you would have them do unto you.*

However, when the other person has a much different worldview from yours, the *Platinum Rule* trumps the Golden Rule:

*Do unto others as they would have you do unto them.*

The Platinum Rule tells us that people view the world differently, having diverse understandings and styles. When you work with people from different cultures or generations, you cannot use your own baseline of experience to judge how they will react.

More specifically, if you are from the United States and you are working with colleagues from Japan or India or Great Britain, you have different traditions and protocols. The same is true with people from different generations within the same country.

Something that you do quite naturally with colleagues from your own generation could be quite offensive to a business associate who is much older or much younger than you are.

In this chapter, you review three types of diversity: *cultural*, *generational*, and *personal*. So let's get started.

## Cultural Diversity:

### Do You Use a *Direct* or an *Indirect Style*?

Cultures differ in important ways, and one dimension is *context,* the unspoken cultural norms and rituals. To start, think of a culture as being either *low context* or *high context.*

In *low context* cultures, such as the United States:

- People interact with few rituals—communication is somewhat informal and not very structured.

- People use a **direct style** to communicate: the *words* are more important than the situation.

In *high context* cultures, which includes most other cultures around the globe:

- People follow shared protocol which defines how they will interact. Communication is more structured and more formal.

- People use an **indirect style** to communicate: the situation helps define the encounter; thus, the words alone may not convey the meaning of the communication.

People from low context cultures, such as the U.S., tend to use a *direct style* of communication. People who use a direct style get right to the point and can feel comfortable speaking in a highly personal way, even with strangers. In business settings, direct communicators get down to business quickly, dismissing small talk until they finish the deal.

In contrast, people from high context cultures use an *indirect style* and generally communicate in an impersonal way at first; anything too personal can be highly offensive. For example, people from high context cultures, such as Japan, South America, India, and some parts of Europe, prefer to follow formal protocol, especially in the beginning. Getting down to business too quickly can put off people from high context cultures. Indirect communicators include a lot of small talk until they develop trust and respect, then they are ready to do business.

In fact, even in the U.S., various segments of the country differ in their communication styles. Northerners tend to be more direct than Southerners, and people from the Northeast tend to be more direct than people from the Midwest.

Indirect communicators can mistake direct communication as being rude; in contrast, direct communicators can be impatient with indirect communication. When people communicate using diverse styles, the situation is ripe for misassumptions.

People who communicate indirectly place a high value on being polite, and asking questions directly sometimes feels rude. For example, indirect communicators may exchange two or three messages before actually stating their question, making their request or saying exactly what they mean. Direct communicators, on the other hand, can become frustrated with this type of back and forth "banter."

| | |
|---|---|
| **Direct Communicator:** | Please give me one or two times next week that you are available for a phone meeting. |
| **Indirect Communicator:** | What is your availability for a call next week? |
| | |
| **Direct Communicator:** | I don't agree. |
| **Indirect Communicator:** | May I make a suggestion? |

To adapt to cultural diversity, neither judge nor be easily offended. Be patient and give the other person the benefit of the doubt. However, regardless of whether a writer has an indirect or a direct cultural style, clear, concise, and brief messages get the best results.

# Personal Diversity:

## What Is Your *Profile*?

That people have different personalities from each other is no secret. One tool that identifies personality tendencies is the Meyers-Briggs Personality Type Indicator (MBTI), which is based on the psychology of Swiss psychiatrist Carl Jung. The MBTI measures the following:

- How people make decisions
- What energizes people
- How people process information
- What type of structure or order people need to function effectively

According to Trisha Svehla, president of Managing the Mosaic, the MBTI gives excellent insight into personality differences in the workplace.[1] Svehla applies the MBTI in her corporate consulting and training because it offers a logical model of consistent human behavior that emphasizes the value of diversity.

The MBTI provides an objective framework for improving communication patterns by relating how emotional differences can lead to sources of conflict. By understanding differences, co-workers are able to value each member's unique contribution to the team. By understanding their own unique profile, individuals can also manage themselves more effectively in diverse environments.

Though personality type is innate, it is also influenced by the environment. Because behavior is observable, you may be able to identify some of your own personality tendencies simply by reading the descriptions that follow. Here are the four sets of traits:

- Extroverts and Introverts
- Sensors and Intuitives
- Thinkers and Feelers
- Judgers and Perceivers

Though different personality types have different ways of thinking and behaviors, personality type is not an excuse for irresponsible behavior and does not determine a person's potential for success. In fact, people find that as their life circumstances change and they mature, some of their personality tendencies also change.

An effective objective for anyone who has extreme tendencies in a category would be to maintain awareness and find balance. To find more harmony and balance, first accept diversity in other people's communication styles by dropping any judgment. Then be open to adjusting your own style.

As you read each of the four sets of traits, see if you can identify your MBTI profile.

**Extroverts Versus Introverts**     How people relate to others influences how they are energized. Extroverts direct their attention outward toward people and things and have high energy. On the other hand, introverts direct their attention inward towards concepts and ideas; they may have no problem with little social contact for long periods and tend to be private.

Getting energy from socializing, *extroverts*:

- Enjoy talking on the phone
- Act quickly, sometimes without thinking
- Like to have people around in the work environment
- Like to learn a new task by talking it through with someone
- Are often expressive, friendly, and open about themselves
- Will tell you what they think
- Are sometimes impatient with long, slow jobs
- May prefer to communicate by talking rather than writing

Getting energy from being alone, *introverts*:

- Like quiet for concentration; dislike interruptions
- Can work on one project for a long time without interruption
- Are interested in the idea behind the job
- May prefer to learn by reading rather than talking or experiencing
- Must be asked what they think
- Think before they act
- Work alone contentedly
- May prefer communications to be in writing

Regardless of whether you are an extrovert or introvert, writing is not necessarily the best mode of communication when relationships seem strained. Pick up the phone or walk over to a colleague's desk to solve problems before they become issues in the workplace.

**Sensors Versus Intuitives**	How people take in information affects how they perceive the world. While sensors are practical and perceive through the five senses, intuitives direct perceptions through the "sixth sense." Sensors are more aware of things around them and like all the small facts and details, whereas intuitives are abstract and look at the big picture, being future oriented.

Preferring standard operating procedure and focusing on what works now, *sensors*:

- Work steadily, with a realistic idea of how long it will take
- Usually reach a conclusion step by step
- Are careful about the facts; details are important
- May be good at precise work
- Can oversimplify a task
- Accept current reality as a given

Focusing on how things could be improved, *intuitives*:

- Work in bursts of energy powered by enthusiasm with slack periods in between
- May make leaps in thought and jump to conclusions quickly
- Follow their inspirations and hunches
- Are interested in the big picture
- May get their facts a bit wrong; dislike taking time for precision
- Can make a task more complicated than it needs to be
- Are visionary and ask why things are as they are

In writing, the detail that sensors provide may irritate intuitives, who prefer a global view; whereas the lack of attention intuitives give to detail may frustrate sensors.

## Thinkers Versus Feelers
This category reflects the way people judge information as they make decisions.

Tending to make decisions objectively, *thinkers:*

- Need a logical argument to back up a decision
- Seem insensitive to others
- Don't always know when they hurt someone's feelings
- Argue a point for the fun of it
- Do not seem to be hurt easily and are thick skinned

Making decisions on the basis of their feelings or emotions, *feelers*:

- Make decisions more subjectively than objectively
- Are sensitive and more easily insulted—thin skinned
- Prefer to avoid arguments and conflict
- Tend to be warm, gentle, and diplomatic

If you score high on thinking *or* feeling, your writing style will reflect your personality type. Though neither approach is right or wrong, a balanced approach is more effective and easy to achieve.

- *Thinkers* tend to be abrupt, getting right to the point and making little or no effort to connect with the reader as one human to another. Though thinkers resist using niceties, they could balance their writing by using a salutation and closing and including a nicety at times, such as *hope your day is great.*

- *Feelers* tend to include fluff in their writing and seem compelled to say things such as *have a great day* and *thank you.* At times they place as much or more emphasis on connecting to the reader as they do in conveying the information. If you are a feeler, stay to the point and limit fluff. Do not say *thank you* more than once in a message, and say it only in response to someone assisting to you.

Judgers Versus Perceivers    *Judgers* prefer a lifestyle that is planned, decisive, self-regimented, and purposeful; *perceivers* prefer a lifestyle that is spontaneous, curious, flexible, and adaptable.

Working best when they can plan their work, *judgers*:

- Like to get things settled and finished
- May decide things too quickly
- May be truly dependent on schedules and calendars
- Tend to be satisfied once they reach a judgment on a thing, situation, or person
- Want only the essentials needed to begin their work
- Use lists as agendas for action
- Look for control; someone must be in charge

Preferring to leave things open for last-minute changes, *perceivers:*

- Adapt well to changing situations
- May have trouble making decisions, needing more information
- May start too many projects and have difficulty finishing them
- May postpone unpleasant jobs
- Want to know all about a new job
- Accomplish a lot at the last minute under pressure of a deadline
- Use lists as reminders of all the things they have to do someday

If you take the MBTI, your score will reveal your personality type as one of a possible sixteen profiles. By gaining insight into your profile, you may expand understanding and acceptance of people with diverse qualities. You may also gain insight into how your personality style contributes to your writing style.

Next, let's review generational styles, focusing on differences in their use of technology.

# Generational Diversity:

## What Is Your *Generational Style*?

Have you noticed that each generation communicates in its own unique style? Are you aware of how to work with people of different generations to develop trust and respect?

Though sources vary, here is a rough breakdown of the various generations:

- Veterans and Silent Generation, born 1925 to 1945
- Baby Boomers, born 1945 to 1964
- Generation X, born 1964 to 1980
- Generation Y or Nexters, born 1980 to 2000

A major difference in how the various generations communicate is their use of e-communication; though many Veterans and Boomers use e-mail effectively, many still prefer phone calls and face-to-face communication.

Veterans and Boomers are known for *not saying* what is on their minds, but instead *they tend to make people guess*. Veterans and Boomers grew up in eras in which politeness and protocol kept communications running smoothly.

In fact, many still base decisions on protocol, not necessarily how they feel in the moment: Veterans, and Boomers to a lesser extent, were taught that feelings were not relevant when it comes to business, but getting the job done was. As a result, many professional Boomers sacrificed their personal lives for professional careers.

In contrast, younger generations expect to have both: a personal life and a successful career. Boomers do not always understand when younger generations are not willing to make the same sacrifices.

If a personal problem arises with a Veteran or Boomer, take it seriously and deal with it proactively: most of the time you can melt the problem by showing some attention to the issue and respect to the person. When a Boomer acts suspiciously, the real message the Boomer may be sending is "Respect me, and I'll be nice."

*Gen Xers* prefer e-mail and instant messages. In contrast to Boomers, Gen Xers do not make you guess, *they tell it like it is.* Listen to what they have to say and stay connected. Once they speak their minds, you and the Gen Xers should both move on.

Gen Xers are technically savvy, and they use technology to stay connected with friends and family. Gen Xers also play an important role: they provide a bridge between Boomers and Nexters, buffering communication so that misunderstandings are averted.

*Nexters* prefer text messaging, instant messaging, and blogging. Nexters are unique in that *they ask for what they want.* They sound more confident than older generations in the way that they communicate. Though Nexters do not make you guess or wait for you to ask them what is going on; when they do speak up, older generations can interpret Nexters as being disrespectful and abrupt.

On the job, Nexters expect the newest technology, and they use it constantly to stay connected with friends and family. When Nexters ask for information, they are more interested in getting their answer quickly than in being treated politely.

In contrast, when Boomers or Veterans make a request, they expect to be treated politely. If a Veteran's requests are ignored or treated abruptly, expect a reaction and possibly one that comes in the form of passive-aggressive behavior.

When it comes to Veterans and Boomers, you will fare well by taking Aretha's advice when she said, "*R E S P E C T*—find out what it means to me."

# Learning Styles:

## Are You a *Global* or an *Analytic Learner*?

Do you thrive on detail or prefer only the bottom line? Learning style, similar to personality style, reveals a person's preferences.

- *Global learners* prefer the big picture, and details can frustrate them.
- *Analytic learners* thrive on the details that lead to the big picture.

Can you tell by the above descriptions which type of learner you are? If not, do some Internet research on *learning styles*. Knowing your learning style validates your unique approach and aids you in making effective choices. More importantly, however, knowing the difference between *analytic* and *global* learners gives you one more tool to adapt your writing for your audience.

If you are analytic, you include a great amount of detail in your writing. Because you appreciate the detail, you may have difficulty understanding how your reader may find the detail distracting. You see, too much detail frustrates global learners, especially when they cannot see where the detail is leading.

Learning styles, like other elements of diversity, are somewhat programmed into our DNA, making change difficult but not impossible. The first step is to be aware of your own style and then to understand the needs of your polar opposite.

Once again, the time to shape your writing for your audience is when you edit, not when you compose. By putting purpose up front, you make your message accessible for all readers, but especially global learners. However, if you still cling to *unnecessary detail*, expect to have difficulty cutting, but do it anyway for your readers.

## COACHING TIP
## Understanding the Concept of *Face*

*Face* plays a prominent role in Hispanic, Asian, and Middle-Eastern cultures, among others. Face affects the measure of one's status, good name, and good character. However, *face* is much more than personal pride.

Face is a concept that:
- Involves the entire group: family, school, workplace, city, and country
- Keeps relationships intact
- Preserves group harmony and promotes group solidarity
- Measures social standing of the person within the group and the social standing of the group

Key attributes associated with *face* include:
- Being honest but tactful
- Being kind without being weak
- Expressing honor and integrity

Behaviors that can be associated with promoting a *lack of face* include:
- Asking questions in a large meeting
- Speaking up in groups
- Challenging authority
- Saying "no" frankly to friends
- Criticizing parents or elders

Though *face* is much deeper and stronger than personal embarrassment, everyone, at some time, feels the impact of shame from making a mistake or anger when blamed is involved.

So how does understanding the concept of *face* contribute to writing more effectively? By understanding diverse styles, a writer is not only more able to adapt to a broad range of styles but also less likely to feel offended when issues arise relating to diversity of styles.

When communication feels challenging, consider *passing the olive branch* so that issues involving face, shame, or blame dissolve more easily.

# Recap

Communication is like a dance: each generation and personality type dances differently. By not reading too much into the meaning behind the style, you will encounter fewer obstacles.

When you do encounter obstacles, mirror your client's behavior and style. Mirroring amplifies similarities: similarities enhance relationships while differences help create a wedge. Here are points to remember:

1. All types are good—preferences are neither right nor wrong.
2. Preferences are much like being right- or left-handed. One feels more natural and effective than the others.
3. As life develops, the environment can influence the direction preferences take.

# Action Steps

What are your *takeaways*? What key points do you plan to apply?

_____

_____

_____

_____

# References

1. Trisha Svehla, President, Managing the Mosiac, is an expert in workplace diversity; go to www.managingthemosaic.com.

2. Science Education Resource Center at Carlton College, <http://serc.carleton.edu/NAGTWorkshops/earlycareer/teaching/learningstyles.html>, accessed May 29, 2009.

# 11

# Write to Influence

As you write to influence or persuade, you may think that the writing itself should create a magical effect: there must be a way to write about your ideas, products, or services so that they garner sudden recognition or sell.

However, the closest you will ever get to creating magic with your words is to write with simplicity and clarity, explaining how your solution solves your client's problem. In fact, all writing that is simple, engaging, and understandable holds persuasive value.

Writing to influence is a *process* involving listening, reflecting, analyzing, and creating. As a process, persuasive writing unfolds: you get closer to the answers you seek by asking questions that help you connect your product with your client's needs. Therefore, this chapter presents questions to help you draw those connections.

A critical element of persuasive writing is credibility because credibility builds trust. To be credible, writing must be correct as well as clear and concise. To enhance your writing further, format your document so that your reader can see your message at a glance. As you review Chapter 13, *Format like a Pro*, you learn the tools and techniques of *visual persuasion*. In other words, persuasive writing is not complete until it is packaged properly, which visual persuasion helps you achieve.

Now let's wrap our thinking around writing to influence—one of the most challenging types of writing, if not the most challenging.

# What Is Persuasion?

Persuasion affects the way people feel, think, and act. When you write persuasively, you write to prompt understanding, action, and commitment.

Right now, you may equate persuasive writing with *formal persuasion*, which is getting a client to adopt an idea, product, or service; but that kind of persuasion in business occurs far less often than *informal persuasion,* the type of persuasion you use in your daily communications.

- **Informal persuasion** is an everyday (and often overlooked) activity shown in the way you interact with coworkers and customers. You use informal persuasion in memos and e-mail.

- **Formal persuasion** is less common and used in client letters and proposals as well as formal presentations to customers and co-workers.

Informal persuasion involves developing good client relationships as a matter of daily business. Strengthening relationships with clients leads to deeper *trust*: the central quality of successful business relationships.

# What Is Informal Persuasion?

With clients, you are using persuasion informally when you call or send an e-mail for updates on progress and satisfaction. With co-workers, you are using persuasion informally when you present ideas at a team meeting, linking them to team and corporate objectives.

At times, persuasion involves human gestures, such as offering an *apology*. When someone's feelings have been hurt or tensions run high, informal persuasion can bring the relationship back in check.

To some, the willingness to say "I'm sorry" demonstrates courage and a humble ego. Therefore, when you acknowledge a mistake and correct it, you are applying informal persuasion; in the process, you are also likely winning respect and gaining trust.

Another time to use informal persuasion is making a complaint. By starting with a positive remark, you are setting the tone and making it more likely the recipient of your complaint will listen with open ears and a soft heart; for example, "I have been a loyal customer of yours for years and have appreciated your products. However, the last shipment was not . . . ." Then, by making your expectations clear, you make it easier for others to accommodate your expectations and bring the relationship back in flow.

An element of informal persuasion is building good rapport; one way to enhance relationships is to show that you appreciate what others do for you. Clients feel your sincerity by something as simple as receiving a thank-you note—all the better if it is handwritten. Also establish deeper trust by having *briefer, more frequent contact*, such as checking in with your client via a phone call or an e-mail message.

Establishing good working relationships with subordinates, supervisors, and customers contributes to success in persuading. *To some extent, you redefine your relationships each day.*

When you take the time to smile and acknowledge others, they notice. When you treat colleagues with respect and kindness, they treat you well in return. In fact, a nurse recently said that she had no idea how important a smile could be until her own mother died. Her emotions were raw and every little gesture of kindness seemed to help her retain her confidence and dignity. She added that only then did she truly realize what a compassionate, empathic way of being might mean to her own patients.

Daily actions contribute more to credibility than education, training, and experience. For example, one small firm in business for more than twenty years has established an extensive client list only through word-of-mouth advertising because its principals have adopted this philosophy: *We promise our clients everything, and then we deliver more than we promise.*

Persuasion tends to be a process that results in a win-win situation, whether it is providing a product that someone needs or getting someone to agree with your point of view; and informal persuasion is the foundation and thus the starting point.

Next, let's look at how you can understand your client so that you can tie your product to your client's needs more effectively.

## What Do Clients Want?

Persuasion is not a one-sided missive: effective persuasive writing integrates the concerns, positions, and needs of your audience. Part of persuasion is developing a genuine concern for your client's needs.

- What are your client's *pain points*?
- What are your client's *expectations*?
- What does your client *value*?

When you communicate to persuade, avoid the common mistake of trying to impress clients with your knowledge or background: clients are interested in you or your company only to the extent that you can help them solve their problems, achieve their goals. Since you have no one to impress, start the process by listening:

- What about your client's situation provokes your empathy?
- What points do you and your client *agree* about?

Identify the *points of agreement*—that is a critical starting point because similarity creates bonds. When you can mirror your client's position, it also shows that you are listening with an empathic ear. Listening and understanding build trust. For example, "I see your frustration, now let's see how we can work together to solve the problem."

Persuasion is not coaxing, encouraging, or trying to get others to do something they do not want to do. When you offer meaningful *benefits* by developing creative *solutions*, your clients see the value in what you have to offer them.

## Who Is Your Client?

Before you bring your proposal to a decision maker (even if that is your own manager), develop your ideas in writing so that they are organized logically.

Start by considering how much your client knows about your product and at what level of complexity.

- Is your client a specialist who speaks the same language as you, having first-hand experience of your product and culture, *or*

- Is your client less familiar and less informed?

One of the biggest mistakes that experts make is explaining their product in a complicated way. *Less is more: simpler is better*. Unless decision makers ask for details, prioritize and simplify information.

At times, decision makers cannot act because proposals do not reflect fundamental courtesies, such as *brevity*. For instance, one large, national commercial real estate corporation sent out an RFP (request for proposal) for a large project and received five proposals: four were an inch and a half thick. The winning proposal was three pages long. The firm's senior vice president remarked, "I didn't even read the long ones. I just didn't have time."

## Will You Be *Direct* or *Indirect*?

Do you need to take a direct or an indirect approach? The difference between the two relates to *context*.

Context helps a reader understand how to evaluate information: context provides details about the *why*.

- A *direct approach* does not present a context: present purpose first and get right to the point.

- An *indirect approach* gives general information about purpose and then develops the *context* for the reader.

Give as many details as necessary, but do not stray from the principle *less is more*. When you need to be indirect, include details to explain the *why* of your idea or product.

## What Is Your *Why* and *How*?

When you write to influence, analyze your information, separating the *why* from the *how*. In general, readers are not interested in learning *how* you are going to achieve your mission until they understand *why*.

For example, think of a time when you were asked to do something but you didn't understand why it was important for you to do it—you couldn't see the value, even if it were something as simple as flossing your teeth. Let's use flossing as an example.

Most people know that flossing is important, but many people still do not floss because "good for your teeth and gums" does not translate into the details of the underlying dynamics: the *why*. The reason to floss is to disrupt the bacteria from creating little ulcerated sores under the gums. Once ulcers are formed, they have an effect on a person's overall health, having recently been linked to heart disease and all sorts of other serious health issues. In fact, flossing is the *only proven way* to heal the ulcers and prevent them recurring—not brushing or gargling or using picks.

Do you think more people would floss if they understood the *why* underneath the *how*? The next step would be to explain the *how* so that flossing correctly becomes achievable and appealing.

Knowing something is not equivalent to believing it. When you can make an issue real by explaining the *why* in a way that ties into personal interests and outcomes, you are closer to achieving results.

## Are *Constraints* or *Resistance* Involved?

Have you ever tried to make a decision listing all the *pros* and *cons* associated with it? The *cons* side of the list is where you will find *constraints* and *resistance*.

- *Constraints* are tangible obstacles, such as an inadequate budget, that inhibit or prohibit a proposal from going forward.

- *Resistance* is intangible, such as a client lacking trust in your product or not seeing the merit in your proposal.

With resistance, emotions are often involved. To dissolve resistance, *ask questions and listen*. Identify the points you both agree on and work outward from those points: agreement is validating—often validation is what a person needs to move forward.

Remain flexible, adapting to your client's needs and showing how your solutions remedy the issues or pain points. Also consider if resistance is in response to your approach:

- Are you too eager about your proposal?
- Could your excitement be pushing others away?
- Are you too busy talking to listen?
- Are you too easily discouraged?

Resistance is unpredictable. You will encounter people sold on your ideas before you even present them as well as those who resist anything new or different without valid reason.

If your client is resisting for valid reasons, do *not* try to talk your client out of his or her position. Forging forward in the presence of valid constraints can create serious, complicated problems and does not lead to long-term, mutually beneficial business relationships.

When a decision maker believes whole-heartedly in a product or idea, nothing can stand in the way from making it happen. If your client favors your proposal, you can be direct and start talking about how to implement it.

To deal with resistance, first identify it. At the right time, produce evidence that your product or service has benefits that exceed the client's reservations: if the concern is that the product is good but not needed, *show how much more effective operations will be if it is adopted.* If decision-makers are attached to a product due to habit, *demonstrate how easy it is to adjust to yours.*

Real reasons for resistance are not easily uncovered, and you will not always have a solution to counteract it. By seeing the situation clearly and then developing an honest response, you know you have done your best regardless of whether you get the business.

## How Can You Motivate Your Client?

Motivation is tied to logic and emotion. You cannot motivate clients by impressing them with your educational degrees, your years of experience, or the company you keep.

Your proposal's value relates to how it benefits your client. In addition to starting your proposal with *points of agreement*, identify specific values and benefits by considering your client's needs. Ask, "What's in it for me?" from your *client's perspective.*

# What Evidence Can You Produce?

Evidence is objective and cuts through bias effectively. For evidence, use data, facts, and figures such as formal and informal research.

Comments from other clients are your most convincing and motivating evidence, for example:

- On your Web site, do you provide an opportunity for clients to provide positive feedback?
- Do you ever ask a client to put their positive words in writing?
- Do you share client success stories with your manager?

---

## Hierarchy of Needs

Psychologist Abraham Maslow 's hierarchy prioritizes needs from the most basic survival needs to the highest level of emotional, intellectual, and spiritual fulfillment.

### Self-Actualization:
*Emotional and spiritual growth*

### Esteem:
*Self-respect and respect for others*

### Social Ties:
*Love, affection, belongingness*

### Safety:
*Security*

### Physiological:
*Physical survival*

In general, humans do not seek to fulfill higher needs while lower needs are threatened. When you are identifying benefits your proposal has for your client, these five broad categories can give insight into the kinds of needs that client addresses. *Where do your ideas fit?*

---

## What Benefits Can You Demonstrate?

Evidence relates to facts; *benefits* relate to the *value* your proposal will produce for your client. A benefit is derived from evidence, both objective and subjective. Translate evidence into benefits:

> When employees improve their skills by 55 percent, they will save approximately 2 hours a day due to improved efficiency. They will also reduce errors by about 20 percent and achieve improved customer satisfaction.

Use your words to paint a picture of how things will look after they adopt your proposal. With the above example, you might say:

> Imagine how relieved you will feel when customer complaints are cut by 20 percent due to improved efficiency. Picture your employees feeling less stress and more satisfaction with their jobs.

Visualizing effectiveness can be more persuasive than using words to *convince* someone about a product's effectiveness.

## Can You Tell a Story?

Storytelling builds context and engages the reader. Here is a traditional story-telling pattern used in persuasive writing: [1]

> Meet George.
> George has a problem and feels pain.
> George tries our solution and now he feels good.
> Would you like to try our solution so that you can feel good like George?

By telling a story, you add a human element to your product.

## Do You Seek Client Input?

Do you use informal persuasion to engage clients in your persuasive process? By giving your clients opportunities to share their ideas, they also lead you to the types of solutions that they need and would find effective.

Collaborating with your clients is the most effective way to develop proposals.

## How Do Listening and Creativity Relate?

Persuasive writing is about solving problems, which relates to creativity. Someone once said that creativity was *listening to the obvious*. For example, have you ever suffered to solve a problem only to find that the answer was right in front of you the whole time?

Listening and creativity both involve *reflection*, a mode of thinking that does not involve *trying* but rather *looking inward* until insight leads to a genuine solution.

The following quote by John Dewey demonstrates why thinking *outside of the box* is so uncommon and difficult to achieve:

> One can think reflectively only when one is willing to endure suspense and to undergo the trouble of searching. To many persons both suspense of judgment and intellectual search are disagreeable; they want to get them ended as soon as possible. They cultivate an over-positive and dogmatic habit of mind, or feel perhaps that a condition of doubt will be regarded as evidence of mental inferiority. . . . To be genuinely thoughtful, we must be willing to sustain and protract that state of doubt which is the stimulus to thorough inquiry . . . .[2]

In other words, immediate answers and quick fixes do not always solve the problem, but they do alleviate the fear looking stupid, at least in the moment. Next, consider what Dr. Ralph W. Tyler said about finding solutions to improve outcomes:

> It's not always what you are doing that you need to do better—sometimes it's what you're not doing at all that you need to begin to do.

Tyler reminds us that trying harder does not always work. Finding an effective solution may mean breaking from the norm, *listening to the obvious,* seeing a situation with fresh eyes, and *boldly going where you've never gone before.*

## What Is Your Plan?

Action comes in stages. Before you actually send a persuasive document, you are likely to have a phone conversation, followed by an e-mail or meeting. Define a plan so that you stay in contact with your client:

- Who are the stakeholders and decision makers?
- What is the time frame?
- What steps can I take to network with my client?

By interacting with your client, you identify the steps to include in your action plan. Use every contact to research your client's needs and identify resistance; use this information to tailor your proposal to your clients and their current circumstances.

Also consider turning ideas on the job into informal proposals. For example, because you have friendly relationships with co-workers, you may not realize the benefit of turning your ideas into informal proposals. Writing is thinking on paper. As you write, ideas become clearer, and you are able to present them more concisely.

Sharing ideas in writing improves their prospect of being adopted: people give ideas more credence when they can mull them over and see how to integrate change. Just as writing and thinking are processes, so is change. In addition, you can address some of your readers' questions before they even ask them, also removing some of the devil's advocate type of challenges.

Try giving team members a copy of your informal proposal, asking for their input before a meeting. You can then incorporate subtle changes and eliminate some concerns *before* your team discusses the merits of your proposed project.

## Recap

By focusing on informal persuasion, you can mold your actions and words to gain support for ideas. By putting your ideas in writing, you can provide evidence and examples to expedite the process.

The key to persuasion is explaining your ideas in a simple, clear, and concise way so that your clients can see how your solution solves their problem. Start with points that your client agrees with and build your proposal from there.

## Action Steps

What are your *takeaways*? What key points do you plan to apply?

# References

1. Lee Lefever, *The Art of Explanation*, John Wiley & Sons, Inc., Hoboken, New Jersey, 2013.
2. John Dewey, *How We Think*, D. C. Health and Company, Massachusetts, 1933, page 16.

# 12

# Develop a Team Charter

Before exploring how writing can influence a team's effectiveness, let's review how easy it is for a team to become dysfunctional. Some pitfalls that can affect a group's effectiveness include:

- Going along to get along: *groupthink*
- Becoming too task oriented too soon
- Letting personal friendships and cliques influence decisions
- Discriminating against teammates (consciously or unconsciously)
- Saying one thing in a meeting and another outside of it
- Being controlling rather than going with the flow

Here are some dysfunctional behaviors that can actually tip team dynamics into the toxic range:

- Undervaluing and interrupting
- Sabotaging
- Shaming and blaming
- One-upping
- Being unwilling to share
- Being disengaged and irresponsible
- Being cynical, negative, and self-involved
- Bullying and gossiping
- *And the list goes on . . .*

At first glance, a successful team might seem to be one in which everyone thinks alike, agrees easily, and makes effortless decisions. However, how teams function when members *disagree* gives more insight into successful teams than when members *seem to agree*.

In fact, the freedom to disagree openly is an important quality of successful teams because a level of trust, honesty, and respect must be present for effective discussions that lead to creative, innovative solutions.

To some extent, teamwork is an extension of cultural mores. For example, the Japanese are known for effective teamwork, but they are also immersed in a culture built around community and collaboration: individuals define their identity through their group more than they do their own personal qualities. In comparison with people from other cultures, Americans tend to be more independent and competitive, immersed in a culture full of diversity and without cultural traditions that support effective teamwork.

For Americans, especially, to work on a team without first clearly defining their plan and strategy—what they expect to achieve, how they will achieve it, and how they will resolve conflict—is a recipe for disaster.

Though an infinite number of ways can turn a group sour, only a few clear paths lead to a synchronicity that produces outstanding results. By developing a *team charter*, a team develops a common understanding that keeps members focused on their mission.

Let's see how professionals can use writing quite literally to *get on the same page*, starting with core questions that define details of a team charter.

## Core Questions

Core questions relate to a team's **purpose**, **plan**, and **results**. By answering core questions, a team develops an identity that gives it a strong power base. In the process, the team also develops objective criteria on which to judge the merit of ideas, taking the onus off the individual. The focus then becomes analyzing how ideas fit into the mission rather than simply arguing a stance; rather than thwarting diverse views, differences can instead be explored, opening the range of possibilities that may lead to real solutions.

Of course, in answering the core questions below, a team would first need to be fully cognizant of how their purpose fits into the broader mission of an organization to which they may belong.

- What is the team's purpose?
- What are the team's processes? How are decisions made?
- What level of participation is expected from each member?
- How does the team give feedback?
- Do team members understand and respect diversity?

Let's take a look at each of these questions, starting with purpose.

Purpose    Too often teams assume their purpose is obvious, so they do not "waste" the time to develop a *purpose statement*—or their mission and vision statements, if that applies.

Instead, they become task oriented too quickly. In fact, focusing on tasks at the expense of defining the group can turn into a form of self-sabotage.

For groups large and small, purpose statements (or *mission* and *vision statements*, if they apply) provide a focus that translates to power, revealing the difference between *what is important* and *what is not*. When groups use these statements to guide their decision-making process, the group's goals, objectives, and action plans have a cohesive baseline to achieve desired results. Only by asking the hard questions does a team develop a cohesive, powerful core.

In fact, until a team has a *clear and unified sense of purpose,* their efforts will be scattered and disagreement will lead to conflict rather than analysis. Only when everyone shares ownership of goals and objectives as well as their importance do teams have the best chance of functioning effectively.

And make no mistake: writing is the *clarifier* and the *unifier.* Only when information is actually written out and shared can there be the possibility of everyone agreeing about the *same thing.* In other words, without clarifying ideas through the writing process, the idea that one person in the room agrees to may be a different idea from everyone else's. Writing clears out the clutter, forces the fine details, and documents the events.

**Processes**     So that team members have clear expectations and boundaries, establish leadership, decision-making strategies, and ground rules early on.

For example, *ground rules* help members understand their boundaries, which also helps them stay on task. When teams write informal *recaps* or formal *minutes* to their meetings, they can establish major decisions as benchmarks. Recaps help ensure that teams move forward consistently toward their goals rather than backtrack to rehash controversial issues. Sending an e-recap prior to the next meeting is a great way to click the "refresh button," getting everyone's focus back on the team's tasks.

By discussing team dynamics openly, members are able to get back in sync before team dynamics suffer.

**Participation**     By clearly understanding expectations, members openly become accountable for their share and quality of work. Accountability translates to a sense of fairness.

**Feedback**    By discussing the difference between constructive feedback and criticism, or even negativity, a team encourages accountability and respect. When members receive constructive feedback, less slacking occurs (also known as *freeloading* or *social loafing*). Members are more likely to become active and engaged—or leave the team (either of which is better than carrying *dead weight*).

By aiming feedback at ideas and processes, not individuals, a team may avert personal attacks. Backbiting, bullying, and scape-goating are destructive and deflate a team's integrity.

**Diversity**    Functional teams respect diversity, understanding the complexities of personal and generational styles.

For example, when diversity is not respected, extroverted team members can easily stifle the quieter, introverted members, putting a lid on creativity and innovation. When generational differences are not understood, diverse styles can easily lead to personal conflict. In contrast, when teams embrace differences in thinking and style, disagreement can lead to deeper understanding and higher quality.

When team members are open and honest during a meeting, they frame issues the same regardless of with whom, when, and where they are speaking. An indication that a team is functional and thus effective is when *team members have the same conversation in the meeting as they do in the hallway after they leave*. In fact, that consistency is also a critical measure of a group's integrity.

Next, let's take a look at *groupthink*, a dynamic that has great potential to derail a group's effectiveness.

# Groupthink

When relationships are more important than mission, a natural result is *groupthink*. Groupthink does not just inhibit creativity—by definition, groupthink prohibits innovative, creative solutions.

When the focus is on relationships rather than mission, fear and insecurity are major drivers in team dynamics, especially for those team members "left out in the cold."

Teams can avert groupthink, in part, by developing a team charter. In the process of developing a team charter, they also put the mission front and center, developing an effective strategy for success.

# Team Charter

Teams can easily fall into the trap of being too task oriented too soon, succumbing to the anxiety of impending deadlines. However, without a plan, team members may not be working on the *right* tasks. This section walks you through the questions that lead to a team charter (see page 172 for a *template* to develop a team charter).

Rather than letting a deadline lead the process, instead start the planning process by establishing a common understanding—*getting everyone on the same page*, so to speak. By establishing purpose and plan up front, a team will have sufficient time to achieve their goals.

To develop cohesion, first define *what* your team will do and then *how* the team will do it. Use questions to reach that common understanding: reframe the basic six questions—*who, what, when, where, why,* and *how*—to establish goals that lead to objectives and an action plan. For example:

- **Goals** are general intentions of what your group will achieve.

- **Objectives** are narrow, precise statements of what your group will do.

Goals and objectives lead to an action plan that consists of tasks along with due dates. If it applies, also be clear about **audience**:

- Who are the decision makers and stakeholders?
- What are their needs and expectations?
- What is their measure of success?

Regardless of how the group collects the details, putting them on paper is important. Recording preliminary discussions through a map or chart establishes progress and aids those whose dominant learning style is visual.

## Purpose, Plan, and Results

Defining your *purpose, plan,* and *results* develops a framework for any type of team project.

### Defining Purpose    *Purpose* embodies the *what* and *why* of the problem: a *purpose statement* defines your project.

1.  *What is your* **purpose statement**? Start by asking, *what is the critical problem that your team is solving?* Then, state the problem and your solution in one sentence.

    For example, if your company has high absentee rates for its employees and your job is to help them solve the problem, your purpose statement might read:

    *Develop a plan to improve employee attendance.*

Develop two or three statements before selecting the best one as your working purpose statement. From a purpose statement, a team can develop goals and objectives, clarify the methods they will use to solve the problem, and even identify the results they will achieve.

2. *What are your **project goals**? What are three to five goals that support your purpose statement?*

   Drawing from the example about employee attendance, here are some goals:

   - Identify root causes of employee absentee behavior.
   - Develop recommendations to management for policy change.
   - Implement a system to improve employee attendance.

Whereas *goals* are broad and somewhat abstract, *objectives* are specific and tangible. By first defining goals, specific objectives can then provide the roadmap to achieving purpose.

3. *What are the team's **objectives**?* After defining goals, identify individual objectives and tasks or action steps. Continuing with the example about employee attendance, here are some objectives relating to the first goal:

   o To identify root causes of employee absence, we need to conduct focus groups, surveys, or individual interviews with employees.
   o To conduct focus groups or survey employees, we need to develop a list of relevant questions.

Based on objectives, tasks will unfold as the team develops *flow* with the project, which you can add to an ongoing *task log*. Use charts with post-it notes: devise your own creative way to keep track of ideas.

## Forming an Action Plan:

### Tasks, Action Steps, and Time Frame

An *action plan* anchors team activities by identifying tangible touchstones to measure progress.

*What are the specific tasks or action steps?* Once you identify tasks, turn them into *action steps* by determining who will complete the task and by what date.

Continuing with the example on employee attendance, here are some action steps:

1. Develop employee survey. (Marcie and Alice; due: May 15)
2. Distribute survey by June 1; collect by June 15. (Joe)
3. Tabulate results. (Joe, Alice, and Marcie; due: June 30)

Your task log will change as your project develops; be flexible in the way that you accomplish your goals. Embrace your team members' unique styles and ways of thinking: use diversity to enrich your project, not destroy it.

### Planning Logistics or Group Operations

At some point early on, identify methods to achieve your objectives by connecting the questions *who, when, where,* and *how* to group operations (logistics), the tasks, and the time frame.

1. *How will we conduct meetings?*

   o How will we establish decisions?
   o What are our ground rules?
   o Will we prepare agendas or keep minutes?
   o How will we keep each other informed (especially if a team member misses a meeting)?

2. *What is the time line?*

   o What is the deadline?
   o What are some milestones or internal deadlines?
   o How often will we meet and where?

3. *What tools or resources do we need to accomplish our tasks?*

   o Do we need laptops, white boards, flip charts, or mapping software?
   o Do we need to develop surveys?
   o Do we need to conduct interviews?

4. *How will know if we are accomplishing our objectives?*

   o How will we give each other feedback?
   o What happens if someone does not fulfill his or her role?
   o What degree of flexibility will we tolerate when someone misses meetings or deadlines?

*What questions does your team need to answer?*

- o   What products will we develop?
- o   What new policies will we implement?
- o   What new skills will employees develop?
- o   How will our outcomes help people, improve systems, or change operations?

You could take the extra step to relate your results to your company's vision or mission. By doing this, you are placing your project in a context, thereby highlighting its importance in a broader scheme. Also, if your research uncovers next steps or leads to new topics to examine, include these in your results.

One final question you may want to ask: *What do team members expect to gain personally from participating?*

The more invested team members are in achieving outcomes, the more driven they will be to achieve group objectives. Teams can nurture individual investment by discussing how members can personally benefit by achieving group goals.

## Team Roles

If a team chooses to assign roles, the most basic roles are *facilitator* and *record keeper*. However, these roles do not need to be static but can change for every meeting. In fact, once a team defines its goals, all members can define clear roles in achieving the team's objectives.

- A **facilitator** leads the group discussion, creating an agenda if feasible. The facilitator can take an active role by collecting ideas on a flip chart or white board; the facilitator directs the discussion by giving one speaker the floor at a time. The facilitator also determines when the group is ready to make a decision or move on to a new topic. Effective facilitators remain objective and use open questions to solicit responses.

- A **record keeper** records decisions and other details, such as information generated on a flip chart or white board. A record keeper would provide a recap or minutes of meetings, presenting them at the beginning of the next meeting or prior to it.

The group can evaluate the meeting by doing a *plus-delta feedback* process at the end of the meeting, which will take perhaps 5 minutes.

---

## COACHING TIP:
## Plus-Delta Feedback

To organize feedback, the evaluator could facilitate a plus-delta activity. The *plus* stands for what worked and *delta* stands for what should be changed. On a flip chart or white board, put a plus sign (+) at the top of one column and a delta sign (Δ) at the top of a second column. First fill in the plus column and then seek to keep balance by putting items in the delta column.

For example:

| + | Δ |
|---|---|
| *The agenda was clear.* | *We spent too much time off topic and should have become focused sooner.* |

---

The goal of the plus-delta feedback activity is to bring the group closer to their ideal, even though the group may not be able to make all of the changes suggested. Members should be realistic about limitations.

If the group wants to delineate roles further, they can appoint a *timekeeper* who would subtly inform the facilitator when time has expired on a topic and the group needs to move on. Another role that could be filled is that of *devil's advocate*, a role that would provide reasons why some of the group's choices might not work as planned.

Always remain aware that special relationships with group members create a situation that is ripe for conflict. Close alliances can cause friction and develop a *split* in the group (that is, even small issues can become controversial, with team members dividing and taking sides). In team activities, treat friends impartially; this boundary helps you maintain trust with other members.

## Ground Rules

During your first or second meeting, take the time to establish *working agreements*, and then periodically revisit them. If you prefer, use the term *guidelines* or *best practices*.

*Here is a starting point for defining ground rules:*

1. Everyone will be open and honest.
2. Everyone will have a say and be heard.
3. Everyone will listen to each other without argument or negative reaction, remaining open and positive.

When conflict occurs, revisit your ground rules and seek agreement among team members to do the following:

- Ask questions to draw out the other side of the conflict.
- Support opinions by facts or examples of specific behavior.
- Listen without judging.
- Avoid interrupting, blaming, and arguing.
- Ask for feedback to check understanding.

- Ask for a commitment to working out a solution.
- Check to see if the group needs training on topics such as diversity, communication, or conflict resolution.
- Set goals, create an action plan, and follow up on your solution.

*What are some other ground rules that would work effectively for your team?*

## Feedback

To keep communication flowing, team members must periodically give each other feedback. Here are some guidelines.

1. *Describe behavior rather than evaluate it.*

   *Describing* relates to giving specific details as to what happened; *evaluating* relates to judging (or criticizing) the behavior. To avoid evaluating, focus on what happened without interpreting the behavior or implying how it affected team dynamics.

   **Evaluating:**   George disrupted the meeting and created problems when he was late.

   **Describing:**   George was 10 minutes late for the meeting.

2. *Be specific rather than general.*

   A general comment does not provide the listener with concrete information, so often the main point remains misunderstood.

   **General:**   You don't treat people with respect.

   **Specific:**   You seemed to interrupt Eunice unnecessarily several times during our last team meeting.

**3.** *Use I statements.*

When giving verbal feedback on challenging issues, shape your words so that you do not sound accusatory. By using an *I statement*, you can keep the focus on how the behavior affected you. Here is a three-part approach for *I statements*:

| | | |
|---|---|---|
| **1.** | How do you feel? | *I feel frustrated* |
| **2.** | Why? | *when I do not receive reports on time* |
| **3.** | Because? | *because I cannot meet my deadlines.* |

Here's another example:

**You statement:**      You are accusing me for the entire problem.

**I statement:**          When I heard that comment, I felt devastated because I felt I was being accused for the entire problem.

Your goal is to keep attention on the behavior and your feelings, and not the person doing it. By speaking about your own feelings, you are more likely to ensure that the other person listens to what you are saying. In addition, people can argue about what seem to be accusations against them, but they cannot legitimately argue with you about your feelings or thoughts.

When a serious issue exists, meet in person and in private. Once again, if you need to document concerns, wait until after you have spoken: you may clarify misunderstandings as you discuss the issues together.

4. *Use the Passive Voice, the Tactful Voice.*

When you communicate about sensitive issues, consider using the passive voice. With the passive voice, you can leave people out of the statement and focus on the issue, which allows those involved to take responsibility or make amends without feeling unduly targeted.

**Active:** You were wrong not to bring the information to the group.

**Passive:** The information should have been brought to the group.

The passive voice is perfect for situations that have the potential to involve blame, for example:

**Active:** You made a mistake on the research.
**Passive:** A mistake was made on the research.

**Active:** You did not inform George about the change.
**Passive:** George was not informed about the change.

When speaking about a problem, the tone sounds less accusatory by not pointing a finger. Not holding someone accountable is an important quality at times.

If you use the passive voice when you give constructive feedback, the listener is more likely hear the message objectively. You can add an *I statement* to further cushion the information.

**For example:** I feel that the decision should have been brought to the entire group.

5. *Turn Negative Feedback into Constructive Feedback.*

The goal of feedback is to change behavior, not to hurt the person receiving it. When you give feedback, be constructive rather than negative.

- **Negative feedback** identifies the problem but not the solution.
- **Constructive feedback** identifies the problem, offers a possible solution, and opens a dialog.

Constructive feedback does not point an accusing finger; it gets the involved persons talking. However, when feedback is conveyed ineffectively, the person receiving it can feel attacked.

*Give PCS Feedback: Positive – Constructive – Supportive*

When you give constructive feedback:

1. Start with an honest, *positive* statement,
2. State the *constructive* feedback, and finally,
3. End on a *supportive* note; for example:

George, you are always so motivated when a project begins, and your motivation adds energy to the project. However, I've noticed that the project is behind schedule because your piece has not yet been completed. Is there anything I can do to assist you?

The way feedback is given (and received) can enhance or destroy a relationship. If you have any doubts about how to convey constructive feedback, role-play the situation.

The best time to address inappropriate behavior is soon after the behavior occurred. However, constructive feedback must also be given at a time when neither the speaker nor the listener feels emotional about it. When people feel emotional, wait until things settle down so that an objective discussion can occur.

**6.** *Avoid Trigger Words.*

Some other words that trigger a negative emotional response are *unsatisfactory, unacceptable, unfair, not, never . . . had enough? Never again . . . .*

**Don't Say:** This research is unacceptable and will not support the project.

**Do Say:** As soon as you are able to find more sources that fit what is needed, we will be able to move forward to the next phase of the project.

Listen with an open mind until you can work through to a win-win solution. Negativity creates a divide and closes the mind to options.

**7.** *Beware of micro-messages: written, spoken, and nonverbal.*

Team members are sensitive to micro-messages: the real message that occurs *between the lines.*

Especially in meetings, be aware of your nonverbal signals. When a member rolls his or her eyes, shrugs shoulders, or nods in disapproval, a dynamic may be set in motion that creates hidden conflict. Even tightly folded arms during a heated discussion give the impression that the listener is closed or angry. Keep your body relaxed and remain aware that your gestures make a difference.

## COACHING TIP: GETTING RESULTS

With communication, recipes usually do not work well. That is because communication must remain interactive; at its best, communication is an interchange, an honest exchange between human beings.

However, since giving constructive feedback can be difficult, here is a pattern to use to keep the discussion focused when addressing something that affects you personally.

First, state the problem and how it affects you; for example:

*When you give me reports late, I cannot complete my work on time, and as a result I feel as if my time is not being respected.*

Next, state what the person can do to solve the problem; for example:

*My request is that you get me the work on time; but when you cannot make the deadline, let me know in advance.*

Finally, open a dialog by asking if the person could change the behavior; for example:

*Could you do that for me?*

Now, think of a current situation and fill in the blanks below.

*When you _____, it makes me feel _____. Therefore, I would appreciate it if you would _____.*
*Would you be willing to _____?*

It takes courage to give and receive constructive feedback, but it can change ineffective behavior and put relationships back on the right track.

# COACHING TIP: RECEIVING FEEDBACK

*When receiving feedback, focus on the content, not on the person.*

1.  Assume the person giving the feedback is concerned about the work, not personal differences.

2.  Focus on the three most common reasons for constructive feedback: to improve skills, quality, or outcomes.

3.  Listen calmly and attentively to get the complete picture.

4.  Tune in fully: your willingness to listen may make the speaker feel better by showing that you are engaged.

5.  Monitor any negative reactions you have to keep them from escalating

6.  Refrain from disagreeing or arguing.

7.  Clarify the feedback by asking a few questions to understand the situation fully; however, avoid antagonizing the person with too many questions.

8.  Acknowledge the other person's concerns, showing that you understand the other person's point of view.

9.  Before responding in detail, ask if you can have some time to reflect upon what you have just learned.

10.  Point to common goals and objectives.

11.  Thank the person for taking the time to discuss the issue with you.

12.  Express your willingness to engage in mutual problem solving.

13.  Reflect on the experience and put it in perspective

14.  Get a good night's rest before you make important decisions.

# Team Writing

From rough draft to final copy, you can do team writing projects in various ways. Here are a few suggestions:

1. *Map out the various parts or sections.* Start with a *concept map* by identifying each major component of the project, creating a visual so that you can see how the pieces fit together. With certain types of documents, such as proposals, standard parts can be identified immediately. (Also note that free mapping software is available online: simply Google, "mind mapping software.")

2. *Research and become familiar with the content and topics.* Fill in details as you go along, using post-it notes or any other creative tool you can devise.

3. *Brainstorm ideas together.* Assign a facilitator to lead brainstorming sessions at any phase of the writing venture. (If feasible, use a laptop, flip chart, or white board).

4. *Coordinate writing assignments with task assignments.* In this way, team members and partners write about tasks they complete and about topics with which they are familiar.

5. *Map pages and compose together or alone.* Mind map each part and turn mind maps into *page maps.* Then compare notes.

6. *Respect differences in learning styles and personality styles.* Some team members work better alone than they do in a group; a team can respect that style through individual tasks rather than forced partnerships.

7. *Establish reasonable due dates.* Team members need to have clear expectations; allow room for error because unforeseen

circumstances can arise—that means setting *internal due dates* in ample time to meet *external due dates*.

8. *Evaluate and revise your draft together:*

   o   Agree up front that every draft will need at least one revision.

   o   Allow time for silent reading *before* discussing a section.

   o   Give suggestions for improving the document rather than criticizing its current state.

9. *Bring the parts together for a final editing.* Write your project in a consistent voice; early on, identify the member who is the most competent writer/editor and reserve that individual's time for the final edit.

10. *Recognize each other for effort that results in work well done!*

Tapping into each other's strengths and then working in constructive ways to get the job done leads to an effective group process.

## Recap

At times, teams have an opportunity to define their own decision-making process. As long as the process is open and consciously developed, a sense of fairness can exist, even when decisions are controversial. However, when decisions are made on the basis of relationships, such as personal friendships and cliques, dishonesty turns into distrust and even hostility. Once a sense of fairness is discarded, group dynamics may forever be dysfunctional.

In effective teams, members discuss controversial issues, stay focused, and remain productive. For participatory groups, members make decisions at a point of consensus, with participants feeling as if their views were heard, respected, and incorporated.

Diversity can enhance creativity and outcomes; however, diverse learning and personality styles can also create challenges for team members to fall into sync with each other. Instead of being springboards for creativity and genuine solutions, differences can become harbingers for mistrust. Here are two points to consider:

- Pushing something under the table and hoping it will go away works best when people are not invested or do not really care.

- Educating a team about diversity, communication, and conflict resolution builds relationships and leads to trust.

Along with embracing diversity, a team develops synergy by defining the group's purpose and processes through a *team charter*, giving the team an identity and a strategy to achieve its objectives.

An indication that a team is functional and thus effective is when *team members have the same conversation in the meeting as they do in the hallway after they leave*. In fact, that consistency is also a critical measure of a group's integrity.

## Action Steps

What are your *takeaways*? What key points do you plan to apply?

# Team Charter Template

Team Purpose | Duration | Timeline

Members

Purpose Statement | Mission Statement

Team Goals

Action Plan (who, what, and when)
     Tasks | Time frame

Workload Distribution

Due Dates

Ground Rules and Guidelines

Resources

Reporting Plan

Outcomes | Results

**To print out a detailed template**:

1. Go to **www.youngcommunication.com**
2. Click on ***The Writer's Toolkit*** tab
3. At The Writer's Toolkit site, click on the ***Templates*** tab.
4. Finally, click on ***Team Charter*** for the template.

# 13

# Format like a Pro

Right now, you may be expending extraordinary effort to craft your message while still overlooking the obvious: *formatting*.

- Formatting speaks to your reader at first glance.
- Effective formatting is *visual persuasion*.

Correct formatting creates professional-looking documents and enhances their credibility. In addition, simple formatting techniques can make key points instantly accessible to readers, improving the appeal of your message. In fact, when you use formatting effectively, formatting becomes an element of your writing style.

One critical element of formatting is *white space*. White space is the blank space on the page that gives readers a chance to rest their eyes, adding a touch of elegance.

At a glance, readers dread bunched up, compacted messages because they appear more complicated. Adding a line of white space in designated places breaks up your message into manageable chunks. To break e-mail messages into short paragraphs, simply leave one blank line between each paragraph (without indenting).

In addition to paragraph breaks and white space, another important visual element is the use of *side headings*. Using bullet points and numbering as well as applying special formatting marks, such as bold, underscore, and italics gives a document visual appeal.

So let's get started.

# White Space and Balance

The term *white space* refers to the unused areas of your document, such as top and side margins as well as spacing between parts and between paragraphs. Official guidelines dictate a range of minimum to maximum spacing to leave between parts.

After you learn official guidelines for spacing, covered on the following pages, you will develop a trained eye for document placement. After you develop a strong visual sense of correct placement, you can selectively break the rules for your own purposes.

White space gives your readers' eyes a place to rest and delineates the various parts of your document. White space also gives readers a place to make notes and comments. White space controls the way your document looks at a glance.

For print documents, use *Print Preview* (located at your *Print* option) and ask yourself the following questions:

- Does this document look balanced, appealing, and professional?
- Does this document look as if it has a picture frame of white space around it?

*Or*:

- Is too much information crowded into too little space?
- Does the document look lopsided or top heavy?

Print documents, such as letters and reports, should look balanced, with top and bottom margins roughly equal. The easiest mistake to make is to leave too little white space at the top of a document, resulting in too much empty space at the bottom.

Side margins should also be equivalent. A professional rule of thumb is to aim for a picture-framed effect. (In general, your default margins will take care of your side margins; however, pay attention to adjusting your print documents vertically.)

E-mail, on the other hand, is less complicated to format. However, e-mail can also look unappealing and thus unprofessional when too little white space is used. Here are some ways to add white space to an electronic document such as an e-mail:

1. Double space (DS) by striking *Enter* (aka *Return*) twice, leaving one blank line.

2. Double space after the salutation.

3. Break your message into short paragraphs. With e-mail, consider that a paragraph can be a sentence or two long.

4. Double space between paragraphs, separating key points for your reader.

5. Double space before and after a closing, such as *Best regards*.

6. Double space after your name, before your automatic sign off.

By adding white space to your e-mail messages, you will achieve a professional-looking message that is also reader-friendly.

## Bullet Points and Numbering

Have you ever received a response to an e-mail in which some of your questions were not answered?

When you have two or more questions, number each question. The reader will have an easier time responding fully to your message. In addition, when you give a list of instructions, number each step.

In professional documents created in a program such as Word, use bullet points to make key points stand out. When you use bullet points, you imply that items are of equal importance; use numbering to prioritize items.

However, with e-messages, you have no idea what kind of device or software program the recipient will use to access your message. Since numbers cross cyberspace intact regardless of the program that your reader uses, numbers are your best choice for e-mail.

Whether you are using bullet points or numbering, apply parallel structure to your lists, which means that you need to represent similar items in the same grammatical form. For example, if you start one item with an active verb, start all with an active verb. If you write one item in a complete sentence, display all in complete sentences.

Experiment using numbering and bullet points and incorporate them as an element of your writing style.

## Formatting Features and Marks

Formatting features include **bold**, <u>underscore</u>, and *italics*; special marks include parentheses and quotation marks. For these elements, follow the guidelines and use them consistently within documents.

Though italics and underscore serve a similar purpose, use italics unless you are writing a document by hand or using a typewriter. That's because in e-writing, the *underscore implies a hyperlink*. In fact, when you write a Web address for hard copy, remove the hyperlink from your document before printing it.

Here are some guidelines for using these special features and marks:

1. *Bold*: Make words stand out by putting them in boldface type.

2. *Italics*: Stress words or give definitions; display book titles or foreign terms in italics.

3. *Quotation Marks*: Enclose direct quotes and technical terms presented for the first time in quotation marks. However, do not use quotation marks to make words stand out because readers

assume the opposite meaning, as in "That's a 'good' idea." (Use single quotation marks within double quotation marks.)

4. *Parentheses*: Put parentheses around information that gives a brief explanation or that does not directly relate to your topic. Also put parentheses around a paraphrase or an abbreviation.

5. *Caps*: Follow traditional capitalization guidelines; do not use all capital letters (all caps) to make words stand out.

All caps connote shouting, so use bold or italics to stress words. Once again, reserve the use of underscoring for indicating hyperlinks.

### How many times should you space after a period?

Though you may have learned to space twice after a period at the end of a sentence, now the correct answer is to *space one time*.

**Here's why:** printing presses have variable spacing, and printers have always left only one space after a period. Since most typewriters did not have variable spacing, typists were instructed to space two times after a period and a colon. However, software programs do provide variable spacing, so the style for spacing is back to where it started centuries ago.

Retraining yourself to space only one time is easier than you may think, and you will be following state-of-the-art guidelines. To a trained eye, writing formatted with only one space after a period or a colon sends the micro-message that the writer is following professional guidelines.

# Side Headings

Most readers find side headings helpful and, thus, documents that include side headings appear more appealing. If you have never used them before, you may not feel comfortable using side headings.

However, notice how you, as a reader, respond when you are reading a document (including this book) that makes use of side headings. If you think that side headings make it easier to understand a document, so will your readers. Readers appreciate every tool that you use to make your document accessible.

Select a part of one of your finished documents. Now see if adding a side heading or two bumps up its appeal and readability. Remember, when you use side headings, apply parallel structure, keeping all headings in the same grammatical form.

# Fonts and Colors

For professional documents, choose conservative fonts such as **Times New Roman** (a *serif* font that creates a pointed look around the edges) or **Arial** (a *sans-serif* font that has uniform thickness and looks flat).

In general, *sans-serif* fonts are easier to read, especially when enlarged. Therefore, use *sans-serif* fonts such as **Arial** or **Calibri**, among others, for PowerPoint presentations and e-communications.

Even though electronic writing allows you to use almost any size font, choose a traditional size. A traditional size for a *serif* font would be 12 points; and for a *sans-serif* font, 10 or 11 points.

Times New Roman is still the font of choice for traditional print documents. Limit the types of fonts you use for any one document to two; for example, if you use Times New Roman for your text, accent titles and side headings with a *sans-serif* font, such as Arial.

The traditional color for print and e-mail messages is black, with blue being a popular alternative for e-mail. However, other colors may detract from your message.

For online documents, you may want to experiment using contrasting colors for side headings, such as blue headings with black print. That combination makes a document attractive and easier to read online than all one color. However, if a document or message looks "too busy," readers can become annoyed: when in doubt, use a conservative design.

Next, let's review vertical spacing, which can be complicated if settings are not correct. The following is a step-by-step guide.

## Paragraph Settings

For formatting guidelines to work, adjust your paragraph settings to the correct starting point. To adjust settings for Microsoft Word:

1. Go to the *Home* tab (located at the upper left corner of your screen).

2. Open the *Paragraph* option by clicking on the arrow.

3. At the *Indents and Spacing* tab, find *Spacing*.

4. Set *Before* and *After* at 0.

5. Set *Line spacing* at *Single*.

6. Click *OK*, so that you are back at the *Home tab*.

7. Set your font at Times New Roman, size 12.

8. Finally, go to the *Page Layout* tab (which is to the right of the Home tab); click on *Margins*, and then select *Normal*.

Once you build your formatting skills, you can add art to science by using your trained judgment to adjust to wider line spacing; however, until you do, you will get the best results by following the guidelines.

# Business Letters: CTA Template

The letter is an excellent vehicle to build business relationships. Your letters represent you and your company, creating an image of both for your client.

Although the purpose and content of letters vary, you can organize most letters successfully by applying the **CTA** template:

1. **Connect**: In the introduction, *connect* with the reader as one person communicating with another. Connect your purpose to the reader's needs and interests; keep the human element present by being friendly rather than stiff and abstract.

2. **Tell**: In the body, *tell* your reader details, explanations, and facts. Summarize and highlight information supporting your purpose.

3. **Act**: In the closing, state the *action needed* or next steps. Express good will; invite the reader to contact you for more information.

*Blocked style* is now the preferred style because of its simplicity (see Figure 10.1); here are the various parts:

1. Letterhead
2. Date
3. Address
4. Salutation
5. Body
6. Closing
7. Writer's name and title
8. Reference initials of typist
9. Enclosure notation
10. Courtesy copy (cc) notation
11. Post script (PS) notation

## Figure 10.1 | Blocked Letter Format

*As you read the letter below, notice how it is formatted—all lines are blocked at the left for efficiency, producing a clean, uncluttered style.*

### Young Communication[1]
180 North Michigan Avenue
Chicago, IL 60611
312-555-1212

July 11, 2011 [2]                    ↓ 4


Mr. Michael Scott [3]
Top-Notch Consultants, Inc.
333 West Hill Street
Los Angeles, CA 90210      ↓ 2 (DS)

Dear Mr. Scott: [4]          ↓ 2

Start your letter by connecting to your reader as one person to another, finding common ground and introducing your purpose.[5]

Let your speech guide your writing. As you provide your reader with details, also do the following:

1. Let clients know that you are committed to helping them achieve their objectives.
2. Feel free to say that you appreciate working with them.
3. Finally, read your letter aloud to ensure that your writing flows as well as your speech does.

In your closing, define *action needed* or *next steps*. Always invite the reader to contact you for additional information.   (DS before the closing.)

Sincerely, [6]                    ↓ 4


Robert Young [7]
Instructional Designer      ↓ 2

djy [8]
Enclosure [9]
cc Elaine Weytkow[10]

PS Use the print preview function to make sure that your letter looks balanced.[11]

# E-Mail Structure: CAT Template

Structure an e-mail message differently from the way that you structure a letter.

Ideally, keep most messages to one screen or less in length. Discuss only one or two main issues in an e-mail; if you need to address multiple topics, consider presenting each main topic in a separate message. Messages that get to the point make it easier for readers to respond.

Here is the **CAT** template:

1. **Connect:** *Connect* as one person to another, keeping a human element in your message. By using the recipient's name as a salutation, you are creating a personal link. Personalize your message further by ending with a short closing.

2. **Act:** Put the requested *action* at the beginning of the message to get the reader's attention. When messages are long, readers do not always read an entire message, saving it for later. For time sensitive messages, list the due date in the subject line. (If time is tight, also make a phone call.)

3. **Tell:** Use the remainder of the message to *tell* your readers key points and essential details.

Although e-mail standards are still evolving, all business writing must follow standard rules for grammar and punctuation; avoid using even standard abbreviations, and never use text messaging language. Though more casual than a business letter, e-mail is a business document that portrays an image of you and your company. Thus, do not be too casual with e-mail.

In other words, to ensure that your documents look professional and appealing, do not use shortcuts to save time.

**Figure 10. 1 | E-Mail Format**

*As you read the message below, notice the spacing guidelines for white space.*

---

To:      **Michael Scott**
Cc:
Subject: **Policy Manual Update**

---

Hi Mike,                    ↓ 2 (DS)

Keep your messages short and put action needed up front.

1.   Create a *personal link* with your reader by using a salutation.
2.   Use visual tools to make your key points stand out.
3.   Number questions so that you get a response to each one.

When you feel unsure about a message, save the message as a draft or make a phone call.

Best regards,              ↓ 2

Bob                        ↓ 2

Robert Young               *Create your automatic sign-off*
Young Communication
180 North Michigan Avenue
Chicago, IL 60611
Phone:   312-555-1212
Fax:     312-555-1234

---

*Note:* Double spacing between parts leaves one blank line between them.

# Draft

The following letter was sent as a follow-up to a meeting. *What changes are made on the revision that enhance the visual appeal and thus the persuasive value?*

---

Dear Helen:

Sally and I enjoyed meeting with you and Mitchell and appreciate the time you spent with us so we could learn about your company. You and your staff have done a great job expanding your business.

I'm sure your background and experience lead you to know how important a good banking relationship is for any company. Since we specialize in commercial banking, we would be glad to help you explore banking and financing opportunities that could benefit your company, such as reducing your costs and giving you more liquidity. We can also provide the capital that you need to meet your growth objectives.

Please feel free to call me at any time. The resources of the First Bank network are here for you to use. We wish you continued success in your company ventures.

Sincerely,

*Steve*

Steve Kroll

---

# Revision

In the following revision, take note of how the writer uses visual tools to make the message more accessible, also making the message more persuasive. *As a reader, which message gains more attention and interest?*

Dear Helen:

We enjoyed meeting you and Mitchell today and learning about your company. You have all done a superb job expanding your business.

You understand the value of a good banking relationship, and we'd like to help you look at banking and financing options to benefit your company. We specialize in serving the commercial banking needs of companies like yours; our products and services can help you:

1. **Reduce** your costs.
2. **Increase** your liquidity.
3. **Provide** the capital you need to meet your growth objectives.

I will call you in the next few days to discuss the possibility of our working together. In the meantime, please call me at (312) 555.1212 if you have questions.

We wish you continued success; thank you again for your time.

Sincerely,

*Steve*

Steve Kroll

## Recap

When you frame your print documents with margins that are beautifully balanced, your readers appreciate your formatting.

Incorporating formatting guidelines for white space into your writing adds a professional finish that enhances its credibility. When you present an effectively finished product, whether print or electronic, all elements work together harmoniously to convey balance and appeal.

## Action Steps

What are your *takeaways*? What key points do you plan to apply?

# 14

# Present Engaging
# PowerPoints

*Death by PowerPoint* results from presenters misusing the purpose of PowerPoint, leading to the abuse of their audiences. Often these are captive audiences diligently working to gain value from a frustrating experience as part of their job. Because let's face it—when audiences are not captive to a situation, they generally leave when they are not getting value.

Even when information is complicated, presenters need to adapt more fully to the needs of their audience. By understanding purpose, presenters can use options to provide complicated information in an engaging way. Though this may take more work in planning and preparation, audiences deserve that respect. Wasting someone's time creates stress. Doing the work up front is what it takes to achieve outstanding results.

However, let no one underestimate the fear and anxiety that someone experiences at the idea of presenting in front of a live audience. Most people go to great extremes to avoid being criticized, and that dynamic can lead to procrastination. By avoiding the inevitable, presenters lose the time that they need to learn their topic, simplify it, prepare supporting material, and develop creative ways to engage their audience.

Let's start with purpose and then walk through a process to help you *prepare*, *practice*, and *present*.

## Respect the Purpose

PowerPoint slides are not meant to tell the whole story. That is the presenter's job. PowerPoint slides should also not be used to present complicated information, that is what additional handouts are for.

Every PowerPoint presentation should aim to engage the audience so that they interact with the information. Otherwise, the presentation is a one-way missive. People do not learn well when information comes to them in a rapid-fire manner—this approach leads to information overload.

Use PowerPoint slides to present key concepts and ideas. After you identify what you want your audience to walk away with, use slides to engage them in a learning process about those key ideas.

By the way, professionals are often relieved when they learn that they will attend an event that does *not* involve a PowerPoint. By relying on flip charts and white boards, a presenter must engage the audience to generate information, which ensures that the event will be interactive. Therefore, even when you prepare a PowerPoint, see if you can also incorporate flip charts and white boards.

The best use for PowerPoint is for short presentations that include large audiences. Even then, though, the presenter needs to be center stage, using slides only to highlight key ideas.

When you learn your topic well enough to teach it in a simple way, your audience will walk away with something they can use, feeling satisfied for time well spent. As Alfred Einstein once said,

"Everything should be made as simple as possible but not simpler."

# Prepare

Prepare your presentation in a systematic manner similar to the way you prepare other forms of communication. Here are steps that lead to effective presentations:

1. Determine the purpose
2. Identify the audience
3. Develop your topic: map it out
4. Choose a design for your slides
5. Sketch our your plan
6. Compose with text and graphics
7. Format each slide
8. Edit text and graphics
9. Prepare your handouts

However, preparing is not a linear, step-by-step process. Working on any part at any time will contribute to the success of the whole.

After you prepare meticulously, you will then be ready to practice and present with ease.

**Determine the Purpose**     Start with your objectives: what do you want to achieve? Think in terms of your topic and your audience.

In the beginning stages of preparing, all of your attention is on your topic because you are still learning it: learning occurs at various levels. Teaching a concept demands learning it at deeper levels.

Therefore, even if you are an expert in an area, you are facing a learning curve that may feel uncomfortable: it is not your topic that is key—it is presenting the topic so that your audience has a learning experience, not just a listening experience.

What do you want your audience to walk away with that they can apply to make their lives or work simpler and more effective?

### Identify the Audience

Who is your audience? How many people will be part of it? What is their background? What are their *pain points*—what is a topic that will help your audience solve some sort of problem? What do they already know about the topic?

- Regardless of the topic, keep it as simple as possible.
- Avoid acronyms and initialisms: even within your corporation, jargon causes confusion.
- Respect cultural differences by using common words, not slang.

Ask a few peers what they think of your topic. By discussing your topic with others, you learn about their experiences, questions, and frustrations, further helping you to mold your topic to the needs of an audience.

### Develop Your Topic: Map it Out

If needed, start by writing about the topic until you can identify your key points. As discussed in chapter 1, develop a mind map, a page map, or even a traditional outline if you know your topic well enough.

Since your presentation is a visual one, consider *storyboarding* to plan your slides. To storyboard, turn your paper horizontally so that its layout is landscape. Then draw a line down the middle, and put your text on one side of the sheet and a sketch of a graphic on the other. In planning your graphics, consider browsing for clip art.

When selecting your graphics, consider the *tone* you wish to convey. For a more professional tone, you might use only photos; whereas for a lighter tone, you might use cartoons. When in doubt, stay conservative. In any case, jot down the image or the file name in your storyboard across from your text.

### Choose a Design for your Slides

Part of planning the organization and content of your slides includes choosing a functional and attractive template. An almost infinite number of designs are available free online.

- Choose a simple theme that will not compete with your message.
- Select colors that contrast to enhance ease of reading.
- Use a non-serif font such as Arial or Calibri because their simplicity makes them easier to read from a distance. (Serif fonts such as Times New Roman are still the best choice for print.)

### Sketch out Your Plan

Transfer the information that you generate from your mind map, outline, or storyboard to slides.

- Decide upon your *major headers*, which will each then be titles for individual slides.
- Create one slide for each major header.
- Divide each header into *sub-topics* or *second-level headers*.
- Divide each of your subtopics further, if necessary.

### Compose with Text and Graphics

Begin to build each slide with the following outcomes in mind.

- Limit the amount of your text to no more than *eight words per line* and *no more than eight lines per slide*; some guidelines recommend even fewer.

- Create a short introduction and a brief conclusion.

- If needed, include *transitional slides* that introduce new sections or summarize what preceded them.

- For large groups, use fewer words and larger print.

- Use animation sparingly: too much animation can be worse than none at all.

The time you are investing will pay off in a multitude of ways—the repetition you go through as you review each slide prepares you to present with confidence.

**Format Each Slide**    As you format, add slides as needed so that your audience can read with ease.

- Set the size of the font so that those in the back of the room can read the slides.

- Break up information and add slides as needed to keep font size readable.

- Include *white space* around your text to improve readability.

- Limit the number of words, the size of your graphics, and the colors you use.

- Keep in mind that light colors may look fine on your computer screen but can seem washed out and be difficult to read when projected on a large screen.

- Be wary of using too many *effects* or changing them too often. Having your words fly in from the left or having slides change like vertical blinds can work well, but mixing too many effects distracts your audience.

**Edit Text and Graphics** As you edit, arrange your slides in a logical order, placing transitional slides appropriately.

- Edit the text and graphics of each slide for accuracy, clarity, consistency, and conciseness.
- Check your facts.
- Cut unnecessary words: *When in doubt, cut it out--less is more.* Cutting is the painful part of editing, but your results are better.
- Use parallel structure, which means present your bullet points in the same grammatical form: noun for noun, verb for verb.
- Use active voice when feasible.
- Eliminate excess graphics.

Finally, make sure that each slide presents information so that everyone in your room can read it easily, regardless of where they are sitting. Your goal is to be concise, clear, consistent, and accurate.

**Prepare Your Handouts** Handouts are not only good tools for your audience, they provide a backup for you in case of any sort of system failure. When you print your slides:

- Select the *Handout* option.
- Select the number of slides per page: 3 to 6 slides allows your audience to take notes effectively.
- Select the *Pure Black and White* option for a crisp, clear copy.

When information becomes complicated, prepare it as a separate handout. Also, to add value to your presentation, consider using a flip chart or whiteboard to collect audience comments, encouraging interaction and adding life to your presentation.

## Practice

Whether 5 people or 100 people are in your audience, do a dry run of your presentation.

The best way to know how you sound is to record yourself. Audio only works well. Listening to your own voice present your topic is the absolute best way to notice subtleties so that you can fine-tune your words.

Listening to yourself also helps you memorize your presentation, building your confidence. In contrast, if you present to a peer, you may find that you are interrupted at key moments, causing needless frustration. And frustration is the last thing you need. If you need to practice in front of someone, hire a professional coach who knows how and when to give feedback.

On the day of your presentation, ensure that good visibility exists in all places in the room. If people cannot read your presentation, you will lose their attention. They will leave disappointed, even if you talk them through it.

## Present

As you speak, consider eye contact and voice as well as your interaction with your slides and audience.

- In a room of 20 to 25 people, make eye contact with everyone at least once throughout the presentation.

- With a large audience, look around as you speak and try to make contact with as many people as possible.

- Since the audience reads slides from left to right, you create a better flow by standing on the right side of the screen (from your audience's perspective).

- As you present, consider your *voice projection, pronunciation, and speed.*

  o Project your voice so that the people in the back of the room can hear it.

  o Practice pronouncing any words that you anticipate having difficulty saying.

  o Modulate your speed—speaking slowly at times and even pausing.

In fact, the faster you speak, the more nervous you are likely to feel.

Do not *hide behind* your slides but rather interact with your slides and audience. Use your slides as part of your *conversation* with the audience: refer to your slides and elaborate on parts of each.

Remember, *reading PowerPoint slides is no more effective than reading a typed speech.*

- Point to the slides and comment on individual terms.
- Interact with the audience by asking questions, regardless of whether you expect an answer.

If you feel confident, include a short activity in which you present the audience with a question; then give them a short time (not more than 5 minutes) to discuss with a partner or small group. However, if you are not confident or prepared enough, you may have difficulty regaining control and the presentation will feel chaotic.

## Recap

Prepare meticulously—do not let your fears hold you back. When you make a mistake, let it go quickly. Only you know what you were "supposed" to say or do.

Even if you have problems with logistics, stay confident and upbeat. Your audience will take your lead. As a wise mother once said, learn how to *act confident* and you will *feel confident*.

In the end, the only one who will give your mistakes a second thought is you—so do not spend any time after your presentation dwelling on what you should have done. If you make a mistake, appreciate the learning opportunity and move on.

The key to doing a great job is preparing well and then going with the flow.

## Action Steps

What are your *takeaways*? What key points do you plan to apply?

# 15

# Apply Best Practices

The vast majority of business professionals have received no training about how to write effective e-mail. Unlike protocol for hard copy correspondence, e-communication continues to mutate and evolve.

Because of these factors, e-mail is not necessarily as easy to manage as professionals sometimes like to think.

## It's Not Personal—It's Business

Has your day ever been ruined because you received an e-mail that sounded accusatory? Or have you ever sent a message that you wish you could have retrieved as soon as you hit the *send* button?

If you find yourself avoiding someone, e-mail should not be your communication mode of choice. Pick up the phone and call the person or walk over to his or her office and have a brief chat. Seeing someone's face or hearing that person's voice can magically melt tension in a way that e-mail cannot. In fact, e-mail has a tendency to perpetuate problems, if not escalate them.

When you feel hurt or reach a point of exhaustion leading you to think that you do not care about outcomes, walk away from the computer. When making your point is more important than how it will affect others, either stop for the day or take a break.

An underlying purpose of all business communication is to build relationships, and that includes e-mail. If you start down a wrong path with a colleague, assert your better side and work to dissolve the issue. Otherwise, you may find yourself losing energy and credibility with your co-workers. You see, negative energy is toxic and spreads like a virus; no one is immune from it.

To keep e-mail use in perspective, always remember that *it's not personal—it's business*. Let's start by reviewing some facts about e-mail, some of which may come as a surprise.

## E-Mail Facts

Over time, you might feel as if your co-workers have become like family and that you are a permanent part of your company. That is not the case, so do not let those cozy feelings lead you to letting your guard down, even if your father owns the company—here is why:

*E-mail messages are official documents and*
*can be used in litigation.*

Always remain aware that your messages can become evidence in legal actions. As a result, your e-mail can also become part of the public domain, as the former employees of Enron discovered. Even casual messages to friends can become part of the litigation process.

*Your computer at work is the property of your organization.*

Your company can—and probably does—monitor your use of e-mail, whether you are aware of it or not. Companies have the legal right to review any messages that you send or receive. In fact, you have no legal right to privacy for any type of Internet usage while at work, even if you are using a personal e-mail account.

*Once you press the send button,*
*your message is out of your control forever.*

Even deleted messages do not go away when they are stored by remote servers. In addition, anyone can forward your message to the CEO of your corporation or a public site. In other words, any e-mail that you send can go around the world; and you can't stop it, even if you know about it. Like any sort of communication, your e-mail message can be twisted and read out of context. And just about anything can go viral in a heartbeat.

We live in a time in which people suddenly find themselves scrutinized by the entire world. Most people who find themselves immersed in notoriety do not expect it to happen . . . until after it has suddenly happened. Then life feels unbearably out of control.

By using technology appropriately, you can avoid heartbreaking scenarios. Do not say or do anything that you would not mind having discussed on the national nightly news or a morning talk show, and you will be safe.

## Best Practices for E-Mail

E-mail does not have rigid rules as compared other types of business correspondence such as letters, memos, reports, and proposals. Though e-mail use continues to evolve, use the following guidelines to keep communications flowing on a professional level:

1.  Start your message with the most important information: put purpose up front and clearly state what you need from the reader.

2.  Respond to e-mail within one or two days, even if you are simply acknowledging that you are working on the request.

3.  Wait about two days after you send a message to follow up on an unmet request or make a phone call.

4. Use an automatic out-of-office response if you will be out of reach for a day or more.

5. Do not Cc people unless they are in the loop. When people are copied unnecessarily, it wastes their time and can send a negative message that creates an awkward situation.

6. Press *reply all* only when you are sure that everyone needs to receive your message; when only the sender needs a reply, other recipients become annoyed because it wastes their time.

7. Include a note at the top of a group message that you send stating that only you should receive a reply. Consider developing group lists in which you show the names but not the e-mail addresses of recipients.

8. Forward messages rather than use Bcc when you want to keep people in the loop; this keeps the communication above board.

9. Use standard capitalization: all CAPS connote shouting; use all lower case only if you are a techie writing to other techies—otherwise, adapt your writing for your audience.

10. Never use text abbreviations in e-mail: *When in doubt, spell it out.* (When you send a message from a mobile device, include a reference such as "Sent from my Blackberry" so your reader does not expect perfection or even a detailed response.)

11. Use an accurate and updated subject line so that your reader can refer to your message and file it easily; include *action needed* in the subject line.

12. Avoid using *read now* and *urgent*; all messages are urgent; demonstrate urgency by using a subject line that includes action needed and a due date.

13. Avoid sending the following types of information via e-mail: confidential, sensitive, or bad news.

14. Encrypt sensitive information such as credit card numbers. (If you do not know how to encrypt information, do a search on "sending sensitive information by e-mail.")

15. Use an *indirect message style* when you must send bad news; however, consider other options before using e-mail.

16. Use visual persuasion so that your reader can pick up key points at a glance; for example, use white space, side headings, bolding, and numbering to enhance your message.

17. Number questions and requests so that they stand out.

18. Add a note at the beginning of forwarded messages: explain the action that the reader should take, or let the reader know that the message is only *FYI* (for your information).

19. Leave the history unless you are certain the reader does not need it; deleted history can create frustration and lost time for your reader.

20. Avoid jargon; however, if you use an acronym or initialism, spell it out the first time, putting the abbreviated form in parentheses: "Include your employee identification number (EID)." Or you can use a less traditional approach, flipping the order: "Include your EID (employee identification number)."

21. Avoid slang, and do not use sarcasm; refrain from sending jokes or being humorous, and use emoticons rarely, if at all.

22. Use e-mail sparingly for personal messages, even if your company allows it.

23. Avoid sounding suspicious, as in "Delete this message upon reading."

24. Avoid saying, "No, that's not our policy," and instead state what you *can do* for a client.

25. Do not respond to controversial or emotional messages unless you are confident and objective; better yet, call the person.

Also, do not copy people simply to CYB (cover your backside); as it sends a negative micro-message that contributes to a lack of trust. The e-mail itself is documentation and needs no additional audience unless you are trying to prove a point, which can easily work against you.

## Recap

At its best, business communication enhances relationships. When communication becomes strained, take a step back and reflect on your options *before* you respond.

*Do not write it if you would not say it face to face.*

When you have done your best and a situation does not seem to be getting better, walk away for a while. Tomorrow is another day, and a good night's sleep refreshes even the worst situation.

When you feel drained of energy, put off making important decisions or writing sensitive messages. Like everyone else, you do your best work when your mind is clear.

## About the Author

Dona Young is a teacher, facilitator, and writing coach who believes that writing is a powerful learning tool and that learning shapes our lives. She has an M.A. from The University of Chicago and is the author of the following trade and textbooks:

*Writing in College: Faster, Better, and Smarter* (2014)

*The Writer's Handbook: A Guide for Social Workers* (2014)

*A Guide for Business Writing*

*The Writer's Handbook: Grammar for Writing*

*The Mechanics of Writing*

*Business English: Writing for the Global Workplace*

*Business Communication and Writing: Enhancing Career Flexibility, 2e*

*Foundations of Business Communication: An Integrative Approach*


And on the lighter side:

*The Princess and Her Gift: A Tale on the Practical Magic of Learning*

*The Little Prince Who Taught a Village to Sing* (with *Andrew's Story*)


For more information, go to **www.youngcommunication.com**.

Made in the USA
Charleston, SC
31 March 2014